TABLE OF CONTENTS

CHAPTER ONE:
WHAT THIS BOOK IS ABOUT

CHAPTER TWO:
THE CONTRACT OF PURCHASE AND SALE

CHAPTER THREE:
FINANCING AND OTHER CONTINGENCIES

CHAPTER FOUR:
PREPARING THE "CORE" TRANSFER DOCUMENTS—THE NOTE, DEED AND MORTGAGE INSTRUMENTS

CHAPTER FIVE:
PREPARATION FOR TITLE ASSURANCE

THE ANATOMY OF
A REAL PROPERTY TRANSACTION
SECOND EDITION

BY
DAVID CRUMP
JOHN B. NEIBEL PROFESSOR OF LAW,
UNIVERSITY OF HOUSTON

AND
JEROME J. CURTIS
PROFESSOR OF LAW
MCGEORGE SCHOOL OF LAW
OF THE UNIVERSITY OF THE PACIFIC

JOHN MARSHALL PUBLISHING COMPANY
c/o DAVID CRUMP
100 LAW CENTER
UNIVERSITY OF HOUSTON
HOUSTON TX 77204
(713) 743-2073
dcrump@uh.edu

Printed in the United States of America.

ISBN: 978-0-916081-02-7

The authors express special appreciation to the following, without whose assistance this book could not have been written:

> LEE HENDERSON and MICHAEL L. RIDDLE of the law firm of Riddle & Brown (upon which the "law firm of Cortelli and Barnes" is based and whose practice includes the preparation of mortgage loan documents used in Arizona, California, Colorado, Illinois, Louisiana, Minnesota, Texas, and Wisconsin); and

> JAMES G. CRUMP of Exxon Chemical Company (upon whom "Edgar Pynes" is based),

with the caveat that the people, events and documents in this book differ in some important respects from the real ones and that any deficiencies in the book are attributable not to them but to the authors.

In addition, the authors wish to thank the following, who provided documents or information: Joyce Langenegger and Ashley Smith of Phillips, King & Smith; Michael Parks of Parks & Moss and Capital Title Company; Michael O'Neal of Village Savings Association; and Susan Perry of the American Land Title Association.

CHAPTER SIX:
THE CLOSING

CHAPTER SEVEN
OWNERSHIP AND RESALE OF THE PROPERTY

CHAPTER ONE:

WHAT THIS BOOK IS ABOUT

A. THE TRANSACTION: EDGAR PYNES BUYS A RESIDENCE

Edgar Pynes was ready to purchase his first home.

This book tells the story of the transaction by which he bought it.

The story begins with a broker, who happened to have an agreement with Park Bank to assist in the sale of certain properties that the Bank had obtained through foreclosure. Negotiations culminated in a contract of purchase and sale. The obtaining of financing, assurance of the title, preparation of conveyancing and mortgage documents, making of escrow arrangements of various kinds, closing of the transaction, recordation, and many other steps followed from the contract.

This book reproduces the major documents and events underlying that transaction. In addition, it gives a hint of subsequent events, including the purchaser's relationship to the homeowners association, restrictions on the use of the property, and the issues that were to arise on resale.

B. WHERE THE TRANSACTION CAME FROM

The events reproduced here are based upon those in a real transaction that was closed recently in Houston, Texas. The deed and mortgage instruments to that transaction (which does differ in some important respects from the one simulated in this book) are recorded among the real property records of Harris County, Texas.

For purposes of this book, the transaction has been transformed into one taking place in the mythical city of "London" and State of "West York," with updated documents. The names of the parties, dates, and other identifying details have been changed, and the transaction itself has been altered in some respects.

C. THE RECONSTRUCTION OF THE TRANSACTION: THE "STATE" OF "WEST YORK"

Our model State of West York has been conceived as a prototype of jurisdictions nationwide, insofar as that is possible. The principal loan documents are forms promulgated by the Federal National Mortgage Association ("Fannie Mae"). They contain many features that are uniform from State to State. In some instances, the actual transaction has been augmented by the insertion of procedures or documents from other States. Finally, since no transaction is completely documented, missing events have been reconstructed from interviews of an actual participant or, when that was impossible, typical procedures have been inserted by simulation.

But the book remains a faithful representation of the basic nature of the transaction. The purchase price is that which was actually negotiated and paid, and many other details of the transaction are pre-

1

served with only identities and details changed. Thus, though parts of what you are about to read have been reconstructed or simulated, we believe the book accurately shows you what a typical real property transaction of this type is like.

D. SOME VARIATIONS TO WATCH FOR

You should keep the following in mind as you consider this transaction.

1. COMPARISON OF THIS RESIDENTIAL PURCHASE WITH A LARGE COMMERCIAL TRANSACTION. How would this transaction differ from, say, the sale of a large apartment complex for many millions of dollars? The answer is that many of the steps would be analogous, although there would be important differences. There would probably be brokerage, a purchase contract, note, deed and mortgage instrument, means of assuring title, and the like, roughly analogous to those steps here. The differences would be reflected in greater complexity and, in some instances, different purposes, in the documents for the apartment transaction (which is really the sale of an ongoing business, with land attached). Throughout the book, we will invite you to compare this residential transaction with a bigger, commercial one.

2. THE ROLES OF PROFESSIONALS, INCLUDING ATTORNEYS. In the eastern United States, attorneys are typically more involved in residential transactions than in western States. In some jurisdictions, an attorney may only prepare closing documents. In others, he may negotiate and draft the sale contract, examine the title, and act as escrow agent and closer. Throughout the book, we will attempt to alert you to these differing roles.

3. JURISDICTIONAL VARIATIONS. In some States, real estate loans are secured by mortgages that are enforceable by judicial sale. In other States, a "deed of trust" or analogous form of mortgage may be used, with a power of private sale. This important difference is one of many that the book will call to your attention through notes.

E. WHY THIS BOOK WILL BE USEFUL TO YOU

This is the biography of a very typical transaction. Neither the property itself nor the process of sale was novel or unusual.

But this, we believe, is precisely its value.

This book will show you characteristic happenings in a typical real property transaction, from beginning to end, with every important document or process set out before you. It recreates a drama that is replayed thousands of times a year in offices throughout America, and what it really shows is the backbone of our system of real property transfer.

Few of the materials in law casebooks are typical. Most are the contested cases that "make" the law. This little book will help you to place that view in context.

Furthermore, it would be a mistake to underestimate this mundane transaction. It provides material for endless debate about the strategy of contract negotiation, the enforceability of financing terms, and many other issues that real estate professionals face every day. It also prompts deeper, more philosophical questions. Should non-lawyer brokers handle the drafting of instruments as representative of both adversary parties? Wouldn't the parties be better protected if each had an attorney? (If so, in a transaction of this nature, would the necessary fees be an excessive percentage of the value of the property?) Should detailed disclosure be required of lenders, or is there an early point at which cost exceeds usefulness? Is our recording system an efficient one upon which to base title assurance? A study of this transaction provides fresh insight into these and other questions.

CHAPTER TWO:

THE CONTRACT OF PURCHASE AND SALE

INTRODUCTORY NOTE

Park Bank had acquired several townhomes and detached homes in the Leebrook Townhouse Subdivision of London, a city in the (imaginary) State of West York. The homes and the subdivision were new. Restrictions on banks usually prevent them from dealing extensively in real property. Furthermore, the properties were unproductive, and Park bank needed to sell them.

At the same time, Edgar Pynes was ready to buy his first home. He was an unmarried man who was about to earn a master's degree in chemical engineering and had a job waiting for him at West York Chemical Company.

The story of their transaction begins with Park Bank's employment of a broker, through the contract excerpted below.

A. BROKERAGE: CONTRACTING FOR THE RIGHT TO SELL

EXCERPTS FROM SELLER'S CONTRACT WITH BROKER
(NOT FOR DRAFTING: USAGE LIMITED TO MEMBER REALTORS)
RESIDENTIAL REAL ESTATE LISTING AGREEMENT: EXCLUSIVE RIGHT TO SELL

[In section 1, the contract identifies the Seller (here, "Park Bank") and the Broker (who is "Betty K. Morris"). * * *

Seller appoints Broker as Seller's sole and exclusive real estate agent and grants to Broker the exclusive right to sell the Property.

2. **PROPERTY:** "Property" means the land, improvements, and accessories described below, except for any described exclusions.

   A. <u>Land:</u> Lot __65_____, Block __2_____, __Leebrook Town House__
   __Subdivision_____ Addition, City of __London_____,
   in __Manero_____County, West York known as __7947 Brainerd__
   __Lane, London, Manero County, West York_____ (address/zip
   code), or as described on attached exhibit.

[The contract continues with detailed descriptions of the attached "Improvements" on the property, from wall to wall carpet to shrubbery, and "Accessories," such as curtains and pool equipment. It then contains a space for listing any "Exclusions" from the list (items that Seller will keep).]

3. **LISTING PRICE:** Seller instructs Broker to market the Property at the following price: $__900,000.00____ (Listing Price). Seller agrees to sell the Property for the Listing Price or any other price acceptable to Seller. Seller will pay all typical closing costs charged to sellers of residential real estate. * * *

4. **TERM:**
   A. This Listing begins on <u>**January 10, 2014**</u> and ends at 11:59 p.m. on <u>**June 30, 2014**</u>.

5. **BROKER'S COMPENSATION:**

   A. When earned and payable, Seller will pay Broker a fee of:

   ☒ (1) <u>**6.0**</u> % of the sales price. * * *

   B. <u>Earned:</u> **Broker's fee is earned when any one of the following occurs during this Listing:**
      (1) Seller sells, exchanges, options, agrees to sell, agrees to exchange, or agrees to option the Property to anyone at any price on any terms;
      (2) Broker individually or in cooperation with another broker procures a buyer ready, willing, and able to buy the Property at the Listing Price or at any other price acceptable to Seller; or
      (3) Seller breaches this Listing. * * *

   E. <u>Protection Period:</u>

      (1) "Protection period" means that time starting the day after this Listing ends and continuing for <u>180</u> days. "Sell" means any transfer of any interest in the Property whether by oral or written agreement or option.

      (2) Not later than 10 days after this Listing ends, Broker may send Seller written notice specifying the names of persons whose attention was called to the Property during this Listing. If Seller agrees to sell the Property during the protection period to a person named in the notice or to a relative of a person named in the notice, Seller will pay Broker, upon the closing of the sale, the amount Broker would have been entitled to receive if this Listing were still in effect. * * *

6. **LISTING SERVICES:**

   ☒ A. Broker will file this Listing with one or more Multiple Listing Services (MLS) by the earlier of the time required by MLS rules or 5 days after the date this Listing begins. Seller authorizes Broker to submit information about this Listing and the sale of the Property to the MLS. * * *

7. **ACCESS TO THE PROPERTY:**
   A. <u>Authorizing Access:</u> Authorizing access to the Property means giving permission to another person to enter the Property, disclosing to the other person any security codes necessary to enter the Property, and lending a key to the other person to enter the Property, directly or through a keybox. To facilitate the showing and sale of the Property, Seller instructs Broker to:
      (1) access the Property at reasonable times
      (2) authorize other brokers, their associates, inspectors, appraisers, and contractors to access the Property at reasonable times; and
      (3) duplicate keys to facilitate convenient and efficient showings of the Property. * * *

   D. <u>Liability and Indemnification:</u> When authorizing access to the Property, Broker, other brokers, their associates, any keybox provider, or any scheduling company are not responsible for personal injury or property loss to Seller or any other person. Seller assumes all risk of any loss, damage, or injury. **Except for a loss caused by Broker, Seller will indemnify and hold Broker harmless from any claim for personal injury, property damage, or other loss.** * * *

[Here, the contract contains several pages of additional provisions, which define default, describe recoverable damages and remedies, provide for mediation, allow a prevailing party in a legal proceeding to recover attorney's fees, and contain several legally required notices.

[In addition, there are several sections in which the seller makes representations and promises to the broker (the seller owns fee simple title, the property violates no laws, the seller will cooperate with the broker, etc.). Also, the broker's liability is limited and the seller agrees to indemnify the broker (from dangerous conditions, acts of third parties, etc.)]

Betty K. Morris		_PARK BANK_	
Broker's Printed Name	License No.	Seller by: _Michael E. Way_	Date
By: _Betty K. Morris_			
Broker's Associate's Signature	Date	Seller	Date

4

Edgar Pynes also consulted a broker. The use of brokers by purchasers is somewhat less frequent than by sellers, although it is also common. Pyne's broker did not enter into a written agreement with him and would look toward division of the fee received by seller's broker for compensation.

B. NOTES AND QUESTIONS ON BROKERAGE

1. REAL ESTATE BROKERS, SALESPERSONS, AND REALTORS®. Real Estate brokers, as the name implies, act as agents in the buying or selling of real property. "Salespersons" or "agents" have more limited functions and must be supervised by brokers. "Realtor" is a registered trademark of certain licensed real estate professionals who are enabled to use the term by the Board of Realtors in their area, who adhere to a code of ethics, and who can offer certain special services (such as the Multiple Listing Service referred to in the contract. See note 5, below.)

2. LICENSING. Most jurisdictions require that real estate brokers be licensed. It is typical for state law to require a broker to prove that he was licensed in order to recover a commission.

3. THE REQUIREMENT OF A WRITING (STATUTE OF FRAUDS). Although the majority of States do not require that a brokerage contract be evidenced by a written agreement, a significant number of States, including several of the most populous, do so require. These States prohibit the recovery of a commission in the absence of a writing. States imposing this requirement vary with respect to the sufficiency of the writing. For example, one can find decisions indicating that a brokerage contract cannot support recovery of the commission if it fails to include a legally sufficient description of the land in question. Is this a sensible requirement? Does it explain why the brokerage contract, above, contains blanks that would prompt the broker to include this information? The writing requirement can be a nuisance to all concerned (particularly if the arrangement changes repeatedly), and it sometimes causes real injustice. But it no doubt also prevents misunderstandings.

4. TYPES OF BROKERAGE AGREEMENTS IN COMMON USE. The contract above is an "exclusive right to sell" form of brokerage agreement. The landowner owes the commission even if he procures the sale himself. Another type of agreement, the "exclusive agency," provides that the broker will be the only agent having a right to act for the landowner, but the landowner may avoid the commission by procuring the sale himself. The "nonexclusive agency" involves the permitted use of multiple brokers, none of whom receives a commission unless he is the "procuring cause" of the sale. The nonexclusive agency has the disadvantage that it may create disputes concerning the procuring cause (indeed, so may the exclusive agency). In residential transactions, the form used here—the exclusive right to sell— is most common. It fully protects the broker. Does it protect the landowner if the broker does not perform? (Hint: the contract provides for the broker to "use reasonable efforts" and "act diligently." Is this an adequate protection? What does "reasonable efforts" mean?)

5. MULTIPLE LISTING SERVICE. The contract itself provides a fairly good introduction to the basic idea of the multiple listing service. The Board of Realtors provides a pooling arrangement to members, by which the listings of any member are available to all, and a commission is divided between the seller's broker and a "cooperating broker" who represents the buyer. (A few courts have held that brokers who are not Realtors must be allowed to use the MLS upon payment of reasonable fees.)

6. THE BROKER'S ENTITLEMENT TO THE COMMISSION. The contract provides, in customary fashion, that the broker's right to the commission attaches when the owner sells or when the broker procures a prospective purchaser "ready, willing and able" to purchase according to the terms in the contract. (Note that the commission is due even if the owner, upon production of a buyer, declines to sell. In a few States, notwithstanding this language, the broker is not normally entitled to the commission unless the sale is actually closed or the seller's refusal is without justification.) The amount of the commission, six percent, is larger than the down payment, as matters turn out. Why? The commission is to be divided, and in this jurisdiction, brokers have more substantial duties than in some other jurisdictions.

7. CONSUMER LEGISLATION: THE BROKER'S CONCERN IN AVOIDING HARM FROM THE

CLIENT. Note the impact of consumer legislation upon the brokerage contract. It goes to considerable lengths to avoid adoption by the broker of misrepresentations by the client. Is the broker's concern in this regard exaggerated?

8. THE TASKS PERFORMED BY THE BROKER. In some jurisdictions, the broker's typical role is limited to procurement of a buyer. In other jurisdictions, including this one, the broker may draw the purchase contract, help obtain financing, arrange the closing, see that required inspections are done, do limited work in clearing titles, arrange title assurance, and, in general, act as a facilitator of the steps that are necessary to close the sale. In States in which brokers' roles are more limited, the roles of attorneys are expanded. Which arrangement is better? (Is it wise for brokers to draft contracts for major purchases? Is is wise for attorneys to arrange termite inspections?)

9. BROKER AS AGENT OF BOTH BUYER AND SELLER. Often, the buyer relies on the broker retained by the seller, who becomes the agent of both. How can a broker "serve two masters?" For example, should the broker tell the buyer that the seller would probably accept $1,000 less than his current offer?

C. NEGOTIATIONS

PURCHASER'S WORKSHEET IN PREPARATION FOR NEGOTIATIONS

7914 Brainerd Lane

Asking price	$ 900,000 reduced to $ 860,000	
My offer	834,200	
Cost?	834,200?	
Down payment	234,200	
To be financed	600,000 if accepted	so: make counteroffer: $ 834,200

NOTE ON NEGOTIATIONS

As a result of the efforts of the brokers, Edgar Pynes looked at several of the townhouses owned by Park Bank, including the one above. He was interested. Negotiations for the possible sale were about to begin.

Negotiation is the "most highly developed skill" exhibited by attorneys, according to Decotiis & Steele, The Skills of the Lawyering Process, 41 Tex. B. J. 483 (1977). The same could probably be said about those who deal professionally in real property.

What techniques are common to negotiation? Concealment of one's settling point exploits the opponent's undervaluing of his position. Inducing the opponent to start the bargaining enhances that effect and enables the negotiator to assemble information from which to infer his opponent's settling point. If he must begin the process, the skilled negotiator will often make an unrealistic offer and couple it with a posture designed to convey an unshakeable conviction that the offer is reasonable. While many people are disinclined to use this approach (and some may see it as unethical), it is in fact so common that it might be viewed as the fundamental negotiating pattern.

In this case, from the seller's point of view, listing at a higher price than one's settling point is good negotiating technique. But in the residential market, the offer must not be too unrealistic or showings to potential buyers might be discouraged. Notice that the purchaser has decided to make a counteroffer lower than the asking price. Should Edgar Pynes, here, have made an even lower offer? Might it have been an effective tactic, in fact, to make an unrealistically low one, in the $700,000 range? (Such an offer

6

might have induced the seller to make a counteroffer from which further negotiations might reduce the price below purchaser's planned offer. In fact Park Bank promptly accepted. The acceptance gives rise to the suspicion that the seller's settling point might have been somewhat lower.)

The result of the negotiations was formalized in the following contract.

D. THE CONTRACT OF PURCHASE AND SALE

EXCERPTS FROM CONTRACT ("EARNEST MONEY CONTRACT")
(NOT FOR USE IN DRAFTING—OFTEN MARKED WITH CHANGES)

1. PARTIES: The parties to this contract are ___Park Bank___ (Seller) and ___Edgar Payne___ (Buyer). Seller agrees to sell and convey to Buyer and Buyer agrees to buy from Seller the Property defined below.

2. PROPERTY: Lot ___65___, Block ___2___, ___Linbrook Town House Subdivision___ Addition, City of ___London___, County of ___Manero, West York___, known as ___7947 Brainerd Lane___ (address/zip code), or as described on attached exhibit, together with: (i) improvements, fixtures and all other property located thereon; and (ii) all rights, privileges and appurtenances thereto, including but not limited to: permits, easements, and cooperative and association memberships. All property sold by this contract is called the "Property".

3. SALES PRICE:
A. Cash portion of Sales Price payable by Buyer at closing .... $ ~~86,000.00~~ 166,840 *EP SM* *changed by agreement EP SM*
B. Sum of all financing described below (excluding any loan funding fee or mortgage insurance premium).. $ ~~774,000.00~~ 667,360 *EP SM*
C. Sales Price (Sum of A and B).. $ ~~860,000.00~~ 834,200 *EP SM*

4. FINANCING (Not for use with reverse mortgage financing): The portion of Sales Price not payable in cash will be paid as follows: (Check applicable boxes below)

☐ A. THIRD PARTY FINANCING: One or more third party mortgage loans in the total amount of $ ~~774,000.00~~ (excluding any loan funding fee or mortgage insurance premium). *667,360 EP SM*
  (1) Property Approval: If the Property does not satisfy the lenders' underwriting requirements for the loan(s), (including, but not limited to appraisal, insurability and lender required repairs), Buyer may terminate this contract by giving notice to Seller prior to closing and the earnest money will be refunded to Buyer.
  (2) Credit Approval: (Check one box only)
  ☒ (a) This contract is subject to Buyer being approved for the financing described in the attached Third Party Financing Addendum for Credit Approval.

* * *

5. EARNEST MONEY: Upon execution of this contract by all parties, Buyer shall deposit $ __8,000.00__ as earnest money with ___SUSIE ALEXANDER___, as escrow agent, at ___COMMONWEALTH TITLE 1800 W LOOP S STE. 700 713.850.8525___ (address). Buyer shall deposit additional earnest money of $_____ with escrow agent within _____ days after the effective date of this contract. If Buyer fails to deposit the earnest money as required by this contract, Buyer will be in default.

6. TITLE POLICY AND SURVEY:
A. TITLE POLICY: Seller shall furnish to Buyer at ☒Seller's ☐Buyer's expense an owner policy of title insurance (Title Policy) issued by ___COMMONWEALTH TITLE OF HOUSTON___. (Title Company) in the amount of the Sales Price, dated at or after closing, insuring Buyer against loss * * *

C. SURVEY: The survey must be made by a registered professional land surveyor acceptable to the Title Company and Buyer's lender(s). (Check one box only)
☒ (1) Within __7__ days after the effective date of this contract, Seller shall furnish to Buyer and Title Company Seller's existing survey of the Property and a Residential Real Property Affidavit promulgated by the Texas Department of Insurance * * * *

D. OBJECTIONS: Buyer may object in writing to defects, exceptions, or encumbrances to title: disclosed on the survey other than items 6A(1) through (7) above; disclosed in the Commitment other than items 6A(1) through (8) above; or which prohibit the following use or activity: _____RESIDENTIAL USE_____

_____.
Buyer must object the earlier of (i) the Closing Date or (ii) __5__ days after Buyer receives the Commitment, Exception Documents, and the survey. Buyer's failure to object within the time allowed will constitute a waiver of Buyer's right to object * * *

7. PROPERTY CONDITION:
A. ACCESS, INSPECTIONS AND UTILITIES: Seller shall permit Buyer and Buyer's agents access to the Property at reasonable times. Buyer may have the Property inspected by inspectors selected by Buyer and licensed by TREC or otherwise permitted by law to make inspections. Seller at Seller's expense shall immediately cause existing utilities to be turned on and shall keep the utilities on during the time this contract is in effect.

B. ACCEPTANCE OF PROPERTY CONDITION: "As Is" means the present condition of the Property with any and all defects and without warranty except for the warranties of title and the warranties in this contract. Buyer's agreement to accept the Property As Is under Paragraph 7B(1) or (2) does not preclude Buyer from inspecting the Property under Paragraph 7A, from negotiating repairs or treatments in a subsequent amendment, or from terminating this contract during the Option Period, if any.
(Check one box only)
☑ (1) Buyer accepts the Property in its present condition.
☐ (2) Buyer accepts the Property in its present condition provided Seller, at Seller's expense, shall complete the following specific repairs and treatments: _____

_____ * * *

8. BROKERS' FEES:
All obligations of the parties for payment of brokers' fees are contained in separate written agreements.

9. CLOSING:
A. The closing of the sale will be on or before _June 30_____, 20_14_, or within 7 days after objections made under Paragraph 6D have been cured or waived, whichever date is later (Closing Date). If either party fails to close the sale by the Closing Date, the non-defaulting party may exercise the remedies contained in Paragraph 15.
B. At closing:
(1) Seller shall execute and deliver a general warranty deed conveying title to the Property to Buyer and showing no additional exceptions to those permitted in Paragraph 6 and furnish tax statements or certificates showing no delinquent taxes on the Property.
(2) Buyer shall pay the Sales Price in good funds acceptable to the escrow agent. * * *

12. SETTLEMENT AND OTHER EXPENSES:
A. The following expenses must be paid at or prior to closing:
(1) Expenses payable by Seller (Seller's Expenses):
(a) Releases of existing liens, including prepayment penalties and recording fees; release of Seller's loan liability; tax statements or certificates; preparation of deed; one-half of escrow fee; and other expenses payable by Seller under this contract.
(b) Seller shall also pay an amount not to exceed $ ___-0-___ to be applied in the following order: Buyer's Expenses which Buyer is prohibited from paying by FHA, VA, Texas Veterans Land Board or other governmental loan programs, and then to other Buyer's Expenses as allowed by the lender.
(2) Expenses payable by Buyer (Buyer's Expenses): Appraisal fees; loan application fees; adjusted origination charges; credit reports; preparation of loan documents; interest on the notes from date of disbursement to one month prior to dates of first monthly payments; recording fees; copies of easements and restrictions; loan title policy with endorsements required by lender; loan-related inspection fees; photos; amortization schedules; one-half of escrow fee; all prepaid items, including required premiums for flood and hazard insurance, reserve deposits for insurance, ad valorem taxes and special governmental assessments; final compliance inspection; courier fee; repair inspection; underwriting fee; wire transfer fee; expenses incident to any loan; Private Mortgage Insurance Premium (PMI), VA Loan Funding Fee, or FHA Mortgage Insurance Premium (MIP) as required by the lender; and other expenses payable by Buyer under this contract. * * *

13. PRORATIONS AND ROLLBACK TAXES:
A. PRORATIONS: Taxes for the current year, maintenance fees, assessments, dues and rents will be prorated through the Closing Date. The tax proration may be calculated taking into consideration any change in exemptions that will affect the current year's taxes. If taxes for the current year vary from the amount prorated at closing, the parties shall adjust the prorations when tax statements for the current year are available. If taxes are not paid at or prior to closing, Buyer will be obligated to pay taxes for the current year.
B. ROLLBACK TAXES: If Seller's change in use of the Property prior to closing or denial of a special use valuation on the Property results in additional taxes, penalties or interest (Assessments) for periods prior to closing, the Assessments will be the obligation of Seller. Obligations imposed by this paragraph will survive closing.

8

14. **CASUALTY LOSS:** If any part of the Property is damaged or destroyed by fire or other casualty after the effective date of this contract, Seller shall restore the Property to its previous condition as soon as reasonably possible, but in any event by the Closing Date. If Seller fails to do so due to factors beyond Seller's control, Buyer may (a) terminate this contract and the earnest money will be refunded to Buyer (b) extend the time for performance up to 15 days and the Closing Date will be extended as necessary or (c) accept the Property in its damaged condition with an assignment of insurance proceeds and receive credit from Seller at closing in the amount of the deductible under the insurance policy. Seller's obligations under this paragraph are independent of any other obligations of Seller under this contract.

15. **DEFAULT:** If Buyer fails to comply with this contract, Buyer will be in default, and Seller may (a) enforce specific performance, seek such other relief as may be provided by law, or both, or (b) terminate this contract and receive the earnest money as liquidated damages, thereby releasing both parties from this contract. If Seller fails to comply with this contract Seller will be in default and Buyer may (a) enforce specific performance, seek such other relief as may be provided by law, or both, or (b) terminate this contract and receive the earnest money, thereby releasing both parties from this contract.

22. **AGREEMENT OF PARTIES:** This contract contains the entire agreement of the parties and cannot be changed except by their written agreement. Addenda which are a part of this contract are (check all applicable boxes):

☒ Third Party Financing Addendum for Credit Approval

☐ Seller Financing Addendum

☐ Addendum for "Back-Up" Contract

☒ Addendum for Property Condition

EXECUTED in multiple originals effective the __10__ day of __April__, __2014__ (BROKER FILL IN THE DATE LAST PARTY SIGNS).

Betty K. Morris _____ 083866000
Listing Broker   License No.

By _Ab Finster_ _____ 082681000
Ann Stormes _____ 082634000
Co-Broker   License No.

Receipt of $ _1000_ Earnest Money is acknowledged in the form of _check_ .

West York Title Insurance Company
Escrow Agent   Date
By _Betty K. Morris_

PARK BANK
Seller _Michael E. Way_
by Vice President
Park Bank Bldg. London 555-6300
Seller's Address   Tel.

Edgar E. Pymes
Buyer
43 Sandra #3A, London 555-5253
Buyer's Address   Tel.

ADDENDA TO THE CONTRACT FOR CREDIT APPROVAL
AND PROPERTY CONDITION

THIRD PARTY FINANCING ADDENDUM FOR CREDIT APPROVAL

[This document begins with a requirement that Buyer "apply promptly for and make every reasonable effort to obtain credit approval for the financing. * * * If Buyer cannot obtain credit approval, Buyer may give written notice within ____ days * * * and this contract shall terminate * * *." The document then tells the parties to "check applicable boxes":]

☑ A. CONVENTIONAL FINANCING:

☑ (1) A first mortgage loan in the principal amount of $ 600,000 (excluding any financed PMI premium), due in full in <u>30</u> year(s), with interest not to exceed <u>4 7/8</u>% per annum for the first <u>5</u> year(s) of the loan with Adjusted Origination Charges as shown on Buyer's Good Faith Estimate for the loan not to exceed <u>1</u> % of the loan.

❑ (2) A second mortgage loan in the principal amount of $_____(excluding any financed PMI premium), due in full in _____year(s), with interest not to exceed _____% per annum for the first _____year(s) of the loan with Adjusted Origination Charges as shown on Buyer's Good Faith Estimate for the loan not to exceed _____ % of the loan.

SELLER'S DISCLOSURE NOTICE (ABOUT CONDITION OF PROPERTY)

[This document begins with a list of possible items, from "cable TV wiring" to "window screens" (Section 1.) Seller is to check boxes for items in or on the property. Then, there follow several pages of possible defects or malfunctions, which the document requires Seller to disclose. The following is an example:

Section 2. Are you (Seller) aware of any defects or malfunctions in any of the following?: (Mark Yes (Y) if you are aware and No (N) if you are not aware.)

Item	Y	N	Item	Y	N	Item	Y	N
Basement		✓	Floors		✓	Sidewalks		✓
Ceilings		✓	Foundation / Slab(s)		✓	Walls / Fences		✓
Doors		✓	Interior Walls		✓	Windows	✓	
Driveways		✓	Lighting Fixtures		✓	Other Structural Components		✓
Electrical Systems		✓	Plumbing Systems		✓			
Exterior Walls		✓	Roof		✓			

If the answer to any of the items in Section 2 is yes, explain (attach additional sheets if necessary): _One window leaked while the deck was being built, but this condition was corrected._____
_____
_____

NOTE: COMPARING THIS TRANSACTION WITH A LARGE COMMERCIAL TRANSACTION

How would these documents differ if the purchase were of a much more valuable property that was expected to produce income? Take, for example, the purchase and sale of a large, operating apartment complex (a common type of transaction for real estate attorneys).

Many of the documents may be closely analogous to those illustrated in later chapters. But there will be important differences.

In particular, the contract of purchase and sale will be far more comprehensive. It will more carefully describe the object of the sale, which will include personalty and possibly intangible property. It will pro-rate and transfer rents, accounts receivable, deposits and the like. It will deal with arrangements for the operation of the business, such as employees and service contracts. Title and related matters will be carefully covered. Ingress and egress, zoning and restrictions, and the possibility of prescriptive or contractual easements will be carefully inquired into. The purchaser will want extensive warranties of title, structural soundness, compliance with law, personalty, and freedom from liens and liabilities (including sales, income or like taxes). It is common for the buyer to demand attachment of financial statements for previous years (as well as tax returns), warranted as to accuracy. The seller, on the other hand, seeks to avoid giving warranties. Inspections may be more extensive: the purchaser, for example, may obtain a rent roll and independently verify it by talking to tenants. Agreement on tax consequences is typically included.

Financing contingencies are typically more carefully explored in a large transaction. The purchaser, buyer, and lender may all, together, enter into a comprehensive single agreement (called, appropriately enough, a "Three-Party Agreement").

In summary, the contract is important. It is the blueprint for the remainder of the transaction. That is so in this modest purchase, just as it is in a much larger one.

NOTE ON THE ROLE OF AN ATTORNEY

This contract was neither drafted nor reviewed by an attorney. Custom varies widely with respect to the roles of attorneys in residential sale contracts. In many jurisdictions, it is customary for the purchaser and seller to sign only an "agreement to agree" until their respective attorneys review any proposed contract. Here is an exemplar:

BINDER

This binder, executed _April 10_, _2014_, confirms my/ our offer to sell and purchase property known as _7947 Brainerd Lane, London, West York_, subject to the following:

1. PURCHASE PRICE: _$834,200.00_
2. DEPOSIT: _$1000.00_
3. FINANCE CONTINGENCY: _30-yr conventional, 20% down, interest not exceeding 4⅞%_
4. CLOSING DATE: _June 30'14 or sooner_
5. ITEMS INCLUDED: _personalty on property_
6. ITEMS EXCLUDED: _none_
7. OTHER PROVISIONS: _seller will not contract with another during 48 hour period hereof_

This binder is subject to execution of a formal Contract of Sale with appropriate attorney review contingency, to be executed within forty-eight hours from the date hereof.

Park Bank by Michael F. Way _____ _Edgar C. Pynes_ _____
Seller _____ Buyer

As a legal document, this "Binder" probably does not "bind;" i.e., it is probably not enforceable as a contract. However, it may serve as a practical means of embodying a good-faith agreement in principle. (Incidentally, does the agreement of the seller not to sell to another during the forty-eight hour period create a legally enforceable option contract? Hint: is it supported by consideration?)

The question remains: Should there be extensive attorney involvement in residential sales contracts? The answer is, it all depends.

A competent attorney will begin with a form that may not differ materially from the one above (if only because an attorney for the other party is likely to insist upon customary phraseology so that he can know what it means). If the attorneys are to be paid fair fees, another expenditure exceeding the down payment may be necessary in this case. There is a significant efficiency loss when it is necessary for two additional professionals to attain a thorough understanding of the transaction. Non-attorneys are likely to see attorneys as creating unnecessary expense for letter-perfect automatically typed documents when a hand-altered, initialed version would do. Attorneys are more likely to kill the deal by nitpicking. The real questions, as a broker might see it, depend not so much on what one could learn in law school but upon a familiarity with the practicalities of real estate customs, with which attorneys are no more familiar than knowledgeable brokers.

But the other side of the coin is the broker's monetary interest in seeing the transaction go through. A broker earns his commission because of the sale, even if it is a poor fit for the parties. The contract printed above is relatively fair to the principals, but even so, it is written so as to protect the broker. Brokers with lesser scruples may use different forms. And isn't there some advantage to drafting or review by an attorney, who (it is to be hoped) knows something about real estate and has been to law school, too? Isn't he/she more likely to deal effectively with the statute of frauds requirement, for example? Finally, consider the importance of the purchase of a residence. It is usually the largest transaction the buyer has ever made, and care should be taken that it is done right.

In the eastern part of the United States, as a crude generalization, attorneys are more extensively involved in residential sales than they are in western States. In the West, the tendency is for attorneys not to be consulted upon contracts for modest residential transactions, and brokers often prepare such contracts.

E. NOTES AND QUESTIONS ON THE CONTRACT OF PURCHASE AND SALE

1. THE FUNCTION OF THE CONTRACT. Since the contract is a blueprint for the rest of the transaction, it should clearly reflect the resolution of any possible dispute. That ideal, however, may be unattainable in practice.

2. "A HOME PURCHASE IS AN EMOTIONAL EVENT." Unsophisticated parties cannot understand all potential disputes well enough to negotiate them thoroughly, and the cost of doing so may be disproportionate. Any contract for a modest residential sale is likely to be a compromise between excessive vagueness and excessive detail. In addition, real estate professionals are fond of saying that a home purchase is not a business deal to the parties. It is an "emotional event."

3. THE REQUIREMENT OF A WRITING. The Statute of Frauds makes the agreement unenforceable unless memorialized by a writing. As in the case of brokerage, the States vary with respect to the required detail. Some States require a relatively specific description of the land (for example, many decisions limit the use of extrinsic evidence to fix boundaries). Notice that the contract describes the addition as "Linbrook," whereas the true name is "Leebrook Town House Subdivision"(!) This error parallels one made by seller's broker in the real transaction. Does it make the contract unenforceable?

4. FINANCING AND OTHER CONTINGENCIES: "PREVAILING" INTEREST RATES, "USUAL" RESTRICTIONS, "CUSTOMARY" CLOSING COSTS, AND THE LIKE. Parties often agree to make the financing contingency depend upon buyer's obtaining a loan at the "prevailing" or "current" interest rate. This convention is used because the parties are usually uncertain of the terms upon which the buyer may be able to obtain a loan. But the lack of specificity may make the contract more difficult for the seller to enforce. There is, strictly speaking, no "prevailing" interest rate, because the rate varies with the lender, borrower, terms, security, and purpose. (The same concern attaches to "usual" encumbrances, "customary" closing costs, and property in "need" of repair.) Note that the financing contingency is reasonably carefully detailed here.

5. "MARKETABLE" TITLE, "GOOD AND INDEFEASIBLE TITLE," OR "INSURABLE" TITLE? A contract may obligate the seller to convey a good title, an insurable title, or a title subject to certain specified outstanding interests. Further, unless the contract provides otherwise, in most States there is implicit in any land sale contract an obligation by the seller to transfer a marketable title. A marketable title is not merely one that can be defended, but one that would not meet reasonable objections from an informed buyer. The language of the contract above does not include an express promise to convey marketable title (but might there be an implied promise to do so?) The contract does call for "a General Warranty Deed conveying title subject only to" specified interests. Does this provision perform the same

function as a marketable title covenant or provide an adequate substitute? Why or why not? Note that the terms of the contract also require a title that an insurer is willing to insure as "good and indefeasible" (or an abstract of title). What does this requirement add to the buyer's protection? Note that, if there are exceptions to or restrictions upon title, the careful procedure is to specify them, because if they are not excepted, the seller may be in breach, or the buyer may consider that he has cause to refuse to close.

6. EXCEPTIONS TO TITLE: THE SELLER'S OBLIGATION. The contract, literally read, does not permit many kinds of encumbrances, and it obligates the seller to cure without the option to terminate. What if an encumbrance is found that is very expensive to cure (a utility easement that is not "usual" for the subdivision)? The literal terms of the contract serve the broker's interest in seeing the deal go through: Literally, it seems, the seller is obligated to buy the easement from the utility!

7. RISK OF LOSS. Paragraph 15 allocates the risk of casualty loss to seller, and, as with title, places upon the seller the obligation of curing before the closing date unless the seller is "unable to do so without fault." This term may place unreasonable obligations upon the seller. It again reflects a preference for completion of the transaction rather than termination.

8. "FURNITURE AND FIXTURES." Personalty not specifically conveyed remains the property of the seller, but "fixtures" are conveyed to the buyer with the rest of the realty. A working definition of fixtures would include items attached to the realty. But there can be disagreements about this concept (for example, is a window air conditioner personalty or realty?) More importantly, such issues can create serious disputes between lay people. When the seller, for example, thinks he has the right to dig up his favorite shrubbery there may be practical difficulties for both sides even though the case law may be clear. The contract deals with the problem by specifying certain common items as realty and by including a blank for "special provisions."

9. DELIVERY OF POSSESSION: LANDLORD-TENANT RELATIONSHIP AT SUFFERANCE. Notice the coverage of the delivery of possession. It is not uncommon for the parties to agree upon a period of occupancy by the seller after closing, depending upon seller's new residence arrangements (it is also not uncommon to make such matters contingencies to the closing). Here, the agreement provides that holdover by the seller shall create a tenancy at sufferance. This language facilitates the use of eviction proceedings in the case of a seller who will not vacate the property. A provision for very high rent upon holdover may provide additional protection.

10. RECORDING; PASSAGE OF EQUITABLE TITLE. The hornbook law is that the equitable title passes to the purchaser, if the contract is enforceable in equity. Therefore, shouldn't the contract be recorded? If it is not, a dishonest seller might effectively convey title to a bona fide purchaser. In States in which attorneys are extensively involved in residential transactions, recording of the contract is common. This contract, in its present form, could not be recorded because it does not contain the form of acknowledgement required in this jurisdiction.

F. NOTE ON JURISDICTIONAL VARIATIONS

To recapitulate, there are many aspects of this stage of the transaction that vary from State to State. Writing requirements, regulation of brokers, consumer protection legislation, and differing interpretations of contract terms are examples of differences in the law. There are even greater variations in customs.

The roles played by brokers and attorneys in preparing the contract and the use of title insurance or title examination are examples of important custom differences.

CHAPTER THREE:

FINANCING AND OTHER CONTINGENCIES

INTRODUCTORY NOTE

At this point, the contract did not bind the parties to close the transaction. In the terminology of the law of contracts, there were certain "conditions precedent" to the obligations at closing. Real estate professionals usually refer to these conditions as "contingencies". The usual practice is for the contract to be subject to such contingencies, because agreement on the blueprint for the transaction usually precedes detail work in assuring the title and obtaining financing. Once the contract is formed, each party may be under an implied obligation to exercise good faith in doing what he reasonably can to remove the contingencies.

The most obvious contingency, here, is financing. The contract obligates the buyer to apply for a loan within five working days. Edgar Pynes applied to Huntington Savings Association, an institution located in his city, and this chapter tells the story of the financing he ultimately obtained.

A. NEGOTIATIONS WITH THE LENDER

LOAN APPLICATION

BORROWER				CO-BORROWER			
Name EDGAR E. PYNES		Age 26	School Yrs 18	Name		Age	School Yrs

BORROWER

Present Address ☐ Own ☒ Rent No. Years

Street 43 SANDRA CIRCLE #3A

City/State/Zip LONDON WEST YORK

Former address if less than 2 years at present address

Street 4810 WINTER LN

City/State/Zip RAYTON, N.Y. 77521

Years at former address ☐ Own ☐ Rent

Marital Status ☐ Married ☐ Separated ☒ Unmarried (incl. single, divorced, widowed)

DEPENDENTS OTHER THAN LISTED BY CO-BORROWER NO. ___ AGES ___

Name and Address of Employer
STARTING AT WEST YORK CHEM CO. BOX 45 LONDON, W.Y.

Years employed in this line of work or profession? 0 years
Years on this job 0
☐ Self Employed*

Position/Title ENGINEER

Type of Business CHEMICAL PLANT

Social Security Number*** 462-55-0000

Home Phone 555-5253

Business Phone 474-3381

CO-BORROWER

Present Address ☐ Own ☐ Rent No. Years

Street ___

City/State/Zip ___

Former address if less than 2 years at present address

Street ___

City/State/Zip ___

Years at former address ☐ Own ☐ Rent

Marital Status ☐ Married ☐ Separated ☐ Unmarried (incl. single, divorced, widowed)

Name and Address of Employer

Years employed in this line of work or profession? ___ years
Years on this job ___
☐ Self Employed*

Position/Title ___

Type of Business ___

Social Security Number*** ___

Home Phone ___

Business Phone ___

GROSS MONTHLY INCOME

Item	Borrower	Co-Borrower	Total
Base Empl. Income	$ SEE BELOW **		
Overtime			
Bonuses			
Commissions			
Dividends/Interest	5000		5000
Net Rental Income			
Other† (Before completing, see notice under Describe Other Income below.)			
Total	$ 5000	$	$ 5000

MONTHLY HOUSING EXPENSE**

Rent	PRESENT $	PROPOSED $
First Mortgage (P&I)		$
Other Financing (P&I)		
Hazard Insurance		20
Real Estate Taxes		20
Mortgage Insurance		
Homeowner Assn. Dues		40
Other: RENT/350		
Total Monthly Pmt.	$	$
Utilities	240	60
Total	1350	$ 622

DETAILS OF PURCHASE

Do Not Complete If Refinance

a. Purchase Price	$ 39,200
b. Total Closing Costs (Est.)	2,200
c. Prepaid Escrows (Est.)	-0-
d. Total (a + b + c)	$ 700
e. Amount This Mortgage	(38,000)
f. Other Financing	(-0-)
g. Other Equity	(-0-)
h. Amount of Cash Deposit	(1,000)
i. Closing Costs Paid by Seller	( )
j. Cash Reqd. For Closing (Est.)	200,200

DESCRIBE OTHER INCOME

◁ B–Borrower   C–Co-Borrower

NOTICE:† Alimony, child support, or separate maintenance income need not be revealed if the Borrower or Co-Borrower does not choose to have it considered as a basis for repaying this loan.

	Monthly Amount
	$

IF EMPLOYED IN CURRENT POSITION FOR LESS THAN TWO YEARS COMPLETE THE FOLLOWING

B/C	Previous Employer/School	City/State	Type of Business	Position/Title	Dates From/To	Monthly Income
	WEST YORK UNIVERSITY	LONDON W.Y.	MASTER'S DEGR.		82-84	$
	TEXAFORNIA GAS CO	DUBLIN TEXAFORNIA	CHEMIST		81-82	1,800.

THESE QUESTIONS APPLY TO BOTH BORROWER AND CO-BORROWER

If a "yes" answer is given to a question in this column, explain on an attached sheet.	Borrower Yes or No	Co-Borrower Yes or No	If applicable, explain Other Financing or Other Equity (provide addendum if more space is needed)
Have you any outstanding judgments? In the last 7 years, have you been declared bankrupt?	No		**WILL OBTAIN SALARY OF APPROX. $12600/MONTH UPON STARTING AT WEST YORK CHEMICAL CO. IN JULY 2014.
Have you had property foreclosed upon or given title or deed in lieu thereof?	NO		
Are you a co-maker or endorser on a note?	NO		
Are you a party in a law suit?	NO		
Are you obligated to pay alimony, child support, or separate maintenance?	NO		
Is any part of the down payment borrowed?	NO		

*FHLMC FNMA require business credit report, signed Federal Income Tax returns for last two years, and, if available, audited Profit and Loss Statements plus balance sheet for same period.

**All Present Monthly Housing Expenses of Borrower and Co-Borrower should be listed on a combined basis.

***Neither FHLMC nor FNMA requires this information.

FHLMC 65 Rev. 8/78   FNMA 1003 Rev. 8/78

This Statement and any applicable supporting schedules may be completed jointly by both married and unmarried co-borrowers if their assets and liabilities are sufficiently joined so that the Statement can be meaningfully and fairly presented on a combined basis; otherwise separate Statements and Schedules are required (FHLMC 65A/FNMA 1003A). If the co-borrower section was completed about a spouse, this statement and supporting schedules must be completed about that spouse also.   ☐ Completed Jointly   ☐ Not Completed Jointly

			Indicate by (*) those liabilities or pledged assets which will be satisfied upon sale of real estate owned or upon refinancing of subject property.			
Description	**Cash or Market Value**		**Creditors' Name, Address and Account Number**	**Acct. Name If Not Borrower's**	**Mo. Pmt. and Mos. left to pay**	**Unpaid Balance**
Cash Deposit Toward Purchase Held By PARK CLIFTON + CO	$ 20,000		Installment Debts (include "revolving" charge accts) WEST YORK BANK + TRUST STUDENT LOAN NOTE		$ Pmt./Mos. /	$ 3,000
Checking and Savings Accounts (Show Names of Institutions/Acct. Nos.) CHECKING ACCT WEST YORK NATIONAL BANK	1,000				/	
Stocks and Bonds (No./Description)					/	
Life Insurance Net Cash Value Face Amount ($ 10,000)	1,800		Other Debts Including Stock Pledges			
SUBTOTAL LIQUID ASSETS	422,800					
Real Estate Owned (Enter Market Value from Schedule of Real Estate Owned)			Real Estate Loans			
Vested Interest in Retirement Fund						
Net Worth of Business Owned (ATTACH FINANCIAL STATEMENT)						
Automobiles (Make and Year) *2005 PONTIAC	7,000		Automobile Loans		/	
Furniture and Personal Property	2,000		Alimony, Child Support and Separate Maintenance Payments Owed To		/	
Other Assets (Itemize)					/	
			TOTAL MONTHLY PAYMENTS		$	
TOTAL ASSETS	432,800		NET WORTH (A minus B) $ 429,500		TOTAL LIABILITIES	B $ 3,000

SCHEDULE OF REAL ESTATE OWNED (If Additional Properties Owned Attach Separate Schedule)								
Address of Property (Indicate S if Sold, PS if Pending Sale or R if Rental being held for income)	◇	**Type of Property**	**Present Market Value**	**Amount of Mortgages & Liens**	**Gross Rental Income**	**Mortgage Payments**	**Taxes, Ins. Maintenance and Misc.**	**Net Rental Income**
			$	$	$	$	$	$
TOTALS →			$	$	$	$	$	$

LIST PREVIOUS CREDIT REFERENCES						
◇ B—Borrower C—Co-Borrower	**Creditor's Name and Address**		**Account Number**	**Purpose**	**Highest Balance**	**Date Paid**
B	WEST YORK BANK + TRUST		# 200011213	STUDENT LOAN	$ 4,500	

List any additional names under which credit has previously been received _____

AGREEMENT. The undersigned applies for the loan indicated in this application to be secured by a first mortgage or deed of trust on the property described herein, and represents that the property will not be used for any illegal or restricted purpose, and that all statements made in this application are true and are made for the purpose of obtaining the loan. Verification may be obtained from any source named in this application. The original or a copy of this application will be retained by the lender, even if the loan is not granted. The undersigned ☐ intend or ☐ do not intend to occupy the property as their primary residence.

I/we fully understand that it is a federal crime punishable by fine or imprisonment, or both, to knowingly make any false statements concerning any of the above facts as applicable under the provisions of Title 18, United States Code, Section 1014.

Edgar E. Pynes

NOTE ON REAL ESTATE LENDING INSTITUTIONS:
SAVINGS ASSOCIATIONS AND HOME MORTGAGE RATES

This application was submitted to "Huntington Savings Association." What is Huntington Savings and what does it do?

REAL ESTATE LENDERS. There are many different kinds of real estate lenders. Banks may be chartered by either the state or federal government. Another kind of depository institution known as savings and loan associations ("S&L's") may likewise be chartered by either kind of government. Still other kinds of depository institutions, called "savings banks" or other names, exist in some States.

In addition to depository institutions, other kinds of lenders participate in real estate transactions. Institutional lenders such as life insurers are frequent lenders in major projects. Mortgage brokers place loans for a fee. Syndications by which equity financing is raised among numerous individual investors is a common means of financing many kinds of ventures, such as raw land purchases or purchases of medium-sized improved properties.

While detailed description of lender regulation is beyond the scope of this book, it is important to state that these different institutions have different functions and are subject to differing statutory and regulatory provisions. As it happens, the institutions most suited to residential mortgage loans are savings and loan associations such as Huntington Savings here. S&L's have historically financed the vast bulk of home purchases in this country.

INTEREST RATES ON FUNDS AVAILABLE TO S&L'S; "THE SQUEEZE." Availability of funds to S&L's has a substantial effect on the residential real estate market. During periods of confidence, low inflation, and available disposable income, S&L's find these funds readily available. During other periods, S&L's are forced, in effect, to ration loans by increased interest rates.

Home loans typically have long terms, exceeding a decade. But the funds borrowed by S&L's have short terms. During certain periods, S&L's have found themselves in a serious squeeze because they had lent funds over long term at low fixed rates but were forced to borrow at relatively high rates. Insolvency worries and necessary mergers have followed. As you will see in these materials, it was important to Huntington Savings (as it is to all lenders) to maintain a reasonable relationship between the income stream on funds they have lent and the outflow on funds they borrow.

NOTE ON LOAN REFUSAL AND REAPPLICATION

Huntington Savings quickly notified Edgar Pynes that it would refuse to lend him the funds he sought. Many S&L's have loan guidelines, designed to assure against default. For example, many insist that loan payments not exceed a certain percentage of the borrower's income (20 to 30 per cent is common). Huntington Savings suggested to Pynes that he might enhance the likelihood of acceptance by obtaining a co-borrower.

Pynes took this advice. He obtained his father's agreement to enter into the transaction with him. This sort of arrangement—sometimes called "rich uncle" financing, in which a relative or close friend incurs indebtedness to assist in the purchase of a home and, at the same time, personally obtains a percentage of equity as an investment—is not uncommon.

S&L's typically act through loan officers, who evaluate prospective borrowers. A loan officer may present an application to the institution's loan committee, with his recommendation. This process is designed to keep the institution's funds working while avoiding bad loans. (The committee usually includes experienced hands at evaluating borrowers .) Once Edgar Pynes had reapplied (with an application identical to his first one, but including his father), his application was approved. In accordance with the loan officer's recommendation, however, the rate would not be the 3.5% applied for; it would instead be 4.625 upon a variable interest rate, or 5% upon a fixed rate. These terms are discussed further below.

NOTE COMPARING THIS RESIDENTIAL TRANSACTION
WITH A LARGER COMMERCIAL TRANSACTION

In a purchase of property for business, investment or development purposes, negotiations with the lender would be far more detailed. The lender would undertake extensive independent appraisal and inspection. Existing lien liabilities would be dealt with by bonds, escrow arrangement, or subordination. The lender would be interested in special provisions protecting the lender's security (such as a "future advance" or "future indebtedness" clause, causing the mortgage to serve as security for additional loans the lender might extend the buyer later). The lender's ability to "call" the note (i.e., declare it due and payable in full) would be the subject of a clause that would be carefully negotiated. Whether the borrower would have personal liability might also be at issue; in some transactions, the lender will agree to look solely to the property for repayment.

B. NOTES AND QUESTIONS ON REAL ESTATE LOAN TYPES (HEREIN OF ARM'S, VRM'S, ROM'S, RAM'S, GPM'S, AND BALLOONS)

1. EDGAR PYNES' LOAN. As is indicated above, Pynes was unable to obtain a fixed-rate mortgage at 3.5 per cent (in fact, he had applied for that rate without much hope of obtaining it). He could borrow at a fixed rate of 5.0 per cent and be assured of the amount of his payments throughout the life of the loan. Or he could use a different kind of borrowing plan.

2. ADJUSTABLE RATE (OR VARIABLE RATE) MORTGAGES ("ARM'S" AND "VRM'S"). If the lender is to take all risk of a fluctuating market, as it does with a fixed rate, it must be compensated for that risk. But if the borrower is willing to share the risk, he can induce the lender to loan at lower rates, and hence the adjustable rate (or variable rate) mortgage. The loan is set at an initial rate, but it is indexed to some measure of the market rate of interest. The borrower's required payments are periodically adjusted accordingly.

3. THE ROLLOVER MORTGAGE ("ROM") AND THE "BALLOON" NOTE. If the borrower is willing to accept a relatively short term, the risk to the lender is correspondingly decreased. The loan may have a term of, say, three to five years, but the payments may be figured as though it were to be repaid over a much longer term of 20, 30 or 40 years. Once the term of the loan has expired, the borrower is liable for all of the balance in one lump sum called a "balloon" payment. It is expected that the buyer will obtain a new loan at that time, reflecting the then-existing interest rate. Usually, the new loan is obtained from the same institution that made the first one, and it is said that the loan is "rolled over." Hence the "rollover mortgage," or ROM. (In the early days, true ROM's involved a contractual obligation to extend, but at an unspecified rate—an arrangement that is now obsolete.)

4. THE GRADUATED PAYMENT MORTGAGE ("GPM"). A graduated payment mortgage involves an artificially lower payment in early years, which is compensated for by higher payments in later years. A chart of payments on a GPM might resemble a flight of steps. (This form of mortgage may be attractive to young professionals who believe their income will increase. Another, more complex, type of mortgage is the Reverse Annuity Mortgage or "RAM", which may be useful to mature borrowers and which is tied to annuity concepts.)

5. RISKS AND BENEFITS OF NON-FIXED RATES. A GPM borrower may see his income suddenly decline and may be unable to meet the increase in his payments. An ARM borrower may find his payments rapidly increasing owing to market conditions. Do the risks outweigh the benefits? Part of the answer is that, with the ARM at least, it is expected that the borrower will indeed benefit, because a fixed rate mortgage, by comparison, has the lender's best estimate of future interest rate behavior built into it— and, in addition, costs the borrower a premium for the lender's bearing of the risks of fluctuations.

6. REGULATION BY THE FEDERAL HOME LOAN BANK BOARD: THE PERCEIVED DANGERS. The Federal Home Loan Bank Board regulates the loans made by savings institutions. It was not until the late 1970's that the Board drafted regulations permitting variable mortgages, and it was not until the 1980's that they became common. About the time of this transaction, one national columnist reported a prediction that "ARM's will clobber the consumer over the next few months." On an average home, an increase from 4 to 5 per cent makes a difference of nearly $500 per month in loan payments; an increase of four per cent, nearly $2000. It is estimated that a two-to-three percent increase in rates could mean as much as a five percent increase in the rate of default upon variable rate mortgages.

7. **"CAPS" ON INTEREST RATE ADJUSTMENTS.** Because of these concerns, some commentators advocate "capping." A "cap" is a limit on increases, preventing the rate from increasing by more than, say, two per cent in any one jump. But a cap somewhat defeats the purpose of the arrangement, because it means that risk is shifted back to the lender, who may not be able to offer the full saving that a variable rate loan saves as versus a fixed one. To the extent that general inflation causes the rate to rise, the buyer has some inherent protection in that, if it is evenly distributed, it will cause a corresponding increase in his earnings. Nevertheless, "caps" are common.

C. LEGALLY REQUIRED DISCLOSURES BEFORE CLOSING

NOTE ON FEDERAL DISCLOSURE REQUIREMENTS

Federal law imposes an elaborate set of disclosure requirements upon residential lenders both before and at closing. As of the date of this writing, lenders must furnish prospective borrowers with (1) a pamphlet promulgated by the Department of Housing and Urban Development explaining the loan process in context, and (2) if the loan is to be sold to federally created entities, a Loan Information Statement, containing descriptions of the lender's practices in narrative form. Within a certain period after the application, the lender must furnish (3) a "Good Faith Estimate of Settlement Charges" and (4) a "Truth in Lending" disclosure form. Also, (5) the Equal Credit Opportunity Act requires a notice.

Portions of these disclosure documents follow. The Truth in Lending Form is not set forth in full because it must be given again at closing unless the loan specifications remain unchanged; therefore, it is dealt with in greater detail in a later chapter, together with other, subsequent disclosure requirements. However, a portion of the Truth in Lending disclosure is reproduced here to remind the reader of its place in the transaction. The reader should consider the probable benefits of these disclosures as well as their probable costs.

LOAN INFORMATION STATEMENT AND GOOD FAITH ESTIMATE OF SETTLEMENT CHARGES (EXCERPTS)

Name of Originator	Borrower
Huntington Savings Association NA	Edgar Pynes and Andrew Pynes
Originator Address	**Property Address**
710 Carillon Parkway St. Petersburg FL 33716	7947 Brainerd Lane London WY 77401
Originator Phone Number (888) 457-5626	**Date of GFE** April 18, 2014
Originator Email	

Purpose	This GFE gives you an estimate of your settlement charges and loan terms if you are approved for this loan. For more information, see HUD's *Special Information Booklet* on settlement charges, your *Truth-in-Lending Disclosures,* and other consumer information at www.hud.gov/respa. If you decide you would like to proceed with this loan, contact us.
Shopping for your loan	Only you can shop for the best loan for you. Compare this GFE with other loan offers, so you can find the best loan. Use the shopping chart on page 3 to compare all the offers you receive.
Important dates	1. The interest rate for this GFE is available through June 30, 2014 12 a.m. After this time, the interest rate, some of your loan Origination Charges, and the monthly payment shown below can change until you lock your interest rate. 2. This estimate for all other settlement charges is available through June 30, 2014. 3. After you lock your interest rate, you must go to settlement within 45 days (your rate lock period) to receive the locked interest rate.

Summary of your loan		
Your initial loan amount is	$ 667,360.00	
Your loan term is	30	years
Your initial interest rate is	4.6250%	
Your initial monthly amount owed for principal, interest, and any mortgage insurance is	$ 2,572.12	per month
Can your interest rate rise?	☐ No ☒ Yes, it can rise to a maximum of 9.6250%. The first change will be in 84 months	
Even if you make payments on time, can your loan balance rise?	☒ No ☐ Yes, it can rise to a maximum of $	
Even if you make payments on time, can your monthly amount owed for principal, interest, and any mortgage insurance rise?	☐ No ☒ Yes, the first increase can be in 85 months and the monthly amount owed can rise to $4,716.37. The maximum it can ever rise to is $5,963.05.	
Does your loan have a prepayment penalty?	☒ No ☐ Yes, your maximum prepayment penalty is $.	
Does your loan have a balloon payment?	☒ No ☐ Yes, you have a balloon payment of $ due in years.	

Escrow account information

Some lenders require an escrow account to hold funds for paying property taxes or other property-related charges in addition to your monthly amount owed of $ 2,572.12

Do we require you to have an escrow account for your loan?

☐ No, you do not have an escrow account. You must pay these charges directly when due.

☒ Yes, you have an escrow account. It may or may not cover all of these charges. Ask us.

Summary of your settlement charges

A	Your Adjusted Origination Charges (See page 2.)	$	1,250.00
B	Your Charges for All Other Settlement Services (See page 2.)	$	15,576.44
A + B	TOTAL ESTIMATED SETTLEMENT CHARGES	$	16,826.44

Understanding your estimated settlement charges

YOUR ADJUSTED ORIGINATION CHARGES

1. Our origination charge This charge is for getting this loan for you.	1,250.00
2. Your credit or charge (points) for the specific interest rate chosen ☒ The credit or charge for the interest rate of 4.6250% is included in "Our origination charge." (See item 1 above.) ☐ You receive a credit of $ for this interest rate of %. This credit reduces your settlement charges. ☐ You pay a charge of $ for this interest rate of %. This charge (points) increases your total settlement charges. The tradeoff table on page 3 shows that you can change your total settlement charges by choosing a different interest rate for this loan.	0.00
A Your Adjusted Origination Charges	$ 1,250.00

YOUR CHARGES FOR ALL OTHER SETTLEMENT SERVICES

Some of these charges can change at settlement. See the top of page 3 for more information.

3. Required services that we select
These charges are for services we require to complete your settlement. We will choose the providers of these services.

Service	Charge
Appraisal fee	400.00
Credit report	35.00
Tax service	83.00
Flood certification	15.00
Verification of Employment Fee	14.00
Appraisal Review Fee	200.00

4. Title services and lender's title insurance This charge includes the services of a title or settlement agent, for example, and title insurance to protect the lender, if required.	1,042.10
5. Owner's title insurance You may purchase an owner's title insurance policy to protect your interest in the property.	4,764.00

6. Required services that you can shop for
These charges are for other services that are required to complete your settlement. We can identify providers of these services or you can shop for them yourself. Our estimates for providing these services are below.

Service	Charge

7. Government recording charges These charges are for state and local fees to record your loan and title documents.	190.00
8. Transfer taxes These charges are for state and local fees on mortgages and home sales.	
9. Initial deposit for your escrow account This charge is held in an escrow account to pay future recurring charges on your property and includes ☒ all property taxes, ☒ all insurance, and ☐ other	5,280.34

21

10. Daily interest charges		
This charge is for the daily interest on your loan from the day of your settlement until the first day of the next month or the first day of your normal mortgage payment cycle. This amount is $85.7372 per day for 14 days (if your settlement is 03/18/2011).		1,103.00
11. Homeowner's Insurance		
This charge is for the insurance you must buy for the property to protect from a loss, such as fire.		
Policy	Charge	
Homeowners Insurance	2,450.00	
		2,450.00
B Your Charges for All Other Settlement Services		$ 15,576.44
A + B TOTAL ESTIMATED SETTLEMENT CHARGES		$ 16,826.44

MULTISTATE
ITEM 73308L2 (C3093L) (100209)

Good Faith Estimate (HUD-GFE)
GreatDocs®
(Page 2 of 3)
00005110000045

DEPICTION OF HUD-REQUIRED BROCHURE:
"SHOPPING FOR YOUR HOME LOAN"

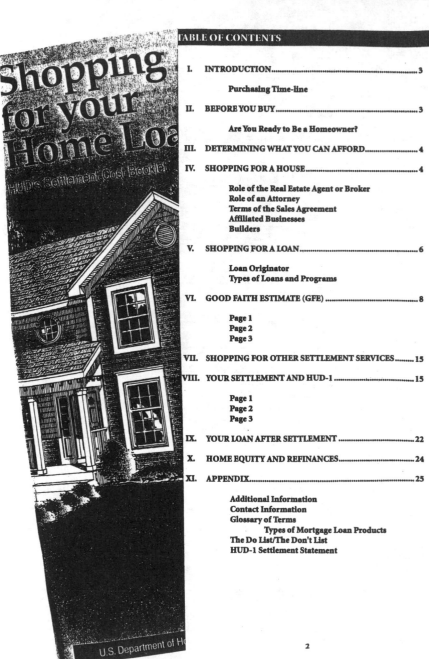

TABLE OF CONTENTS

I. INTRODUCTION

The *Real Estate Settlement Procedures Act (RESPA)* requires lenders and mortgage brokers to give you this booklet within three days of applying for a mortgage loan. RESPA is a federal law that helps protect consumers from unfair practices by settlement service providers during the home-buying and loan process.

Buying a home is an important financial decision that should be considered carefully. This booklet will help you become familiar with the various stages of the home-buying process, including deciding whether you are ready to buy a home, and providing factors to consider in determining how much you can afford to spend. You will learn about the sales agreement, how to use a *Good Faith Estimate* to shop for the best loan for you, required settlement services to close your loan, and the *HUD-1 Settlement Statement* that you will receive at closing.

This booklet will help you become familiar with how interest rates, points, balloon payments, and prepayment penalties can affect your monthly mortgage payments. In addition, there is important information about your loan after settlement, including how to resolve loan servicing problems with your lender, and steps you can take to avoid foreclosure. After you have purchased your home, this booklet will help you identify issues to consider before getting a home equity loan or refinancing your mortgage. Finally, contact information is provided to answer any questions you may have after reading this booklet. There is also a Glossary of Terms in the booklet's Appendix.

Using this booklet as your guide will help you avoid the pitfalls and help you achieve the joys of home ownership.

Purchasing Time-line

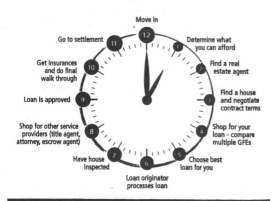

II. BEFORE YOU BUY

Are You Ready to Be a Homeowner?

Buying a home is one of the most exciting events in your life and is likely to be the most expensive purchase that you will ever make. Before you make a commitment, make sure you are ready.

Avoid the pressure to buy a home that you cannot afford. Here are some things to consider:

- Are you ready to be a homeowner? It is critical that you consider whether you have saved enough money to support a down payment in addition to your other debts. You must have job stability and a steady income.

EQUAL CREDIT OPPORTUNITY ACT NOTICE

NOTICE: The Federal Equal Credit Opportunity Act prohibits creditors from discriminating against credit applicants on the basis of race, color, religion, national origin, sex, marital status, age (provided that the applicant has the capacity to enter into a binding contract); because all or part of the applicant's income derives from any public assistance program; or because the applicant has in good faith exercised any right under the Consumer Credit Protection Act. The Federal agency that administers compliance with this law concerning this creditor is: <u>The Federal Home Loan Bank, Dublin, W.Y.</u>

REGULATION Z ("TRUTH IN LENDING") DISCLOSURES

Loan #:   2000001   Property: 7947 BRAINERD LANE, LONDON, WEST YORK 77040

ANNUAL PERCENTAGE RATE	FINANCE CHARGE	Amount Financed	Total of Payments	
The cost of your credit as a yearly rate, which is subject to change.	The dollar amount the credit will cost you, which is subject to change.	The amount of credit provided to you or on your behalf.	The amount you will have paid after you have made all payments as scheduled, based on the current annual percentage rate which may change.	
				Interest Rate
3.5295%	$439,754.86 E	$664,535.20	$1,104,290.06	4.2500 %

Your payment schedule will be:

Number of Payments	Amount of Payments	Payments are Due Monthly, Beginning

[The remainder of the form is omitted because the disclosures are dealt with further in a later Chapter. Since federal law requires mailing of the disclosure within a fixed period of days after application, the lender's attorney followed the practice of retaining a photocopy of the postmarked envelope in which it was sent.]

D. THE LOAN AGREEMENT

COMMITMENT LETTER (LENDER'S PROMISE TO FUND THE LOAN)

Mr. Edgar E. Pynes and Mr. Andrew B. Pynes
43 Sandra Circle # 3A
London, West York 77y040   (commitment no. 110639)

Gentlemen:

We are pleased to inform you that we have approved your application for a mortgage loan, based upon the information that you submitted and other information that we have received about you. The terms of the loan are summarized below:

1. Person(s) to sign Note and Mortgage: <u>Edgar E. Pynes and Andrew B. Pynes</u>
2. Amount of loan: <u>$ 667,360.00</u>
3. Interest rate: <u>4.25 per cent, adjustable (after five years, one year adjustment periods, two point limit, 9.25 point overall limit)</u>

23

4. Term of loan: _____ thirty _____ years

5. Amount of monthly payment: _____ $ 2,125.00 _____, plus a sum to be deposited in escrow for real estate taxes and casualty insurance as described in the mortgage or Deed of Trust.

6. The loan is to be secured by a first mortgage on this _____ one _____-family residence that is (or will be) located at: 7947 Brainerd Lane, London, West York 77040 (which will be called the "Property").

7. We will require you to have hazard insurance on the Property in the amount of ___ $ 667,360.00 ___. You can obtain the insurance from any insurance company that is satisfactory to us. The insurance must name us under what is known as a "mortgage endorsement". Furthermore, the policy must not contain what is known as a "co-insurance" provision. You must also pay the first year's premium and provide us with a receipt for that payment at closing.

8. This loan is given upon condition that the Flood Certificate which you will furnish will show that the property is not in a Flood Hazard Area as defined in the Flood Disaster Protection Act.

9. We will require title insurance and 2 prints of the Survey for the property. Both must be entirely satisfactory to us. In addition, you must furnish the following to the Association's attorney for his review at least 5 business days before the date proposed for closing: (a) Survey, (b) Title Insurance Company Report of Title and Binder, insuring that our mortgage will be a first mortgage in accordance with the Savings and Loan Act, (c) Flood Hazard Certificate satisfactory to the Association, and (d) any other documents required by our attorney.

10. Our attorney will review the commitment for title insurance that you obtain plus the papers prepared by your attorney, if any. The fee for our attorney and all other expenses incurred by you shall be paid by you at or prior to closing.

11. The note, mortgage or deed of trust, and tax letter will be drawn by the association's attorney. All other papers may be drawn by your attorney or, if not, will be drawn by the Association's Attorney.

12. This commitment letter will expire at the close of business on the fifteenth day after the date of this letter, unless we receive from you before then the enclosed copy of this letter, signed by you in the space indicated below. If we receive the signed letter on time, then this commitment letter will not expire until the close of business on July 18, 2014; the loan must be closed by that deadline. Time is of the essence. (If necessary, we will consider extending that deadline, but only if you request us in writing to do so at least two weeks before the deadline.)

13. All matters relating to the loan, must at the time of the closing be entirely satisfactory to us and our attorney. The terms of the loan will be more fully set forth in the Note and the Mortgage.

Please address all correspondence to the attention of the person signing this letter.

REMARKS: This commitment is conditioned upon payment of commitment fee of 2% in advance and other payments required.

The terms of this letter are accepted.

Edgar E. Pynes   4/20/14
Signature of Applicant

Andrew B Pynes   4/21/14
Signature of Applicant

Very truly yours,

HUNTINGTON SAVINGS ASSOCIATION

By: _Cassandra Schwartz_

April 18, 2014

E. OTHER CONTINGENCIES: SURVEY, TITLE COMMITMENT, INSPECTIONS, ETC.

NOTE ON COMMITMENT FOR TITLE INSURANCE

Since the loan commitment is dependent upon receipt of a commitment for title insurance, this commitment is, in effect, one of the contingencies to closing. The title commitment actually appears in Chapter 5, which pertains to title assurance. But the reader should realize that it would actually appear at this point in time sequence.

COVER LETTER ACCOMPANYING ENGINEERING REPORT
(INSPECTION OF STRUCTURAL AND MECHANICAL SYSTEMS)

[The following letter precedes a carefully hedged, room-by-room and system-by-system analysis of the residence. The entire report exceeds twenty-five pages, including pre-printed information and forms for each major system or room.]

Mr. Edgar E. Pynes
43 Sandra Circle, Apt. 3-A
London, West York 77040   Re: 7947 Brainerd Ln., London, W.Y.

Dear Mr. Pynes:

As per your request, this company made a professional inspection of major structural and operable mechanical systems of the structures at the above property on *April 24, 2014.* Any opinions herein are general estimates, and wide variation from the norm is to be expected. * * *

　　　Please remember that systems may be defective although the defect is not observable, and such defects would not be discoverable even by our professional inspection. The building is in generally good condition, considering its age and various pertinent factors, requiring no major repairs and relatively few minor items of repair. Among such items noted were: (1) paint missing in various rooms, as noted in the following report; (2) clothes support bracket in master bedroom closet incomplete; (3) splattered paint on cabinets, walls and floors; (4) lock on bathroom door inoperable; (5) paint on front door incomplete; (6) disposer inoperable; (7) trash in house and yard. * * *

　　　Please read the attached Information Sheet, which is an integral part of the Report, and we remind you that we make no representations regarding inaccessible areas, areas that cannot be tested, or subjects not specifically covered in the Report.

Very truly yours,

SURVEY

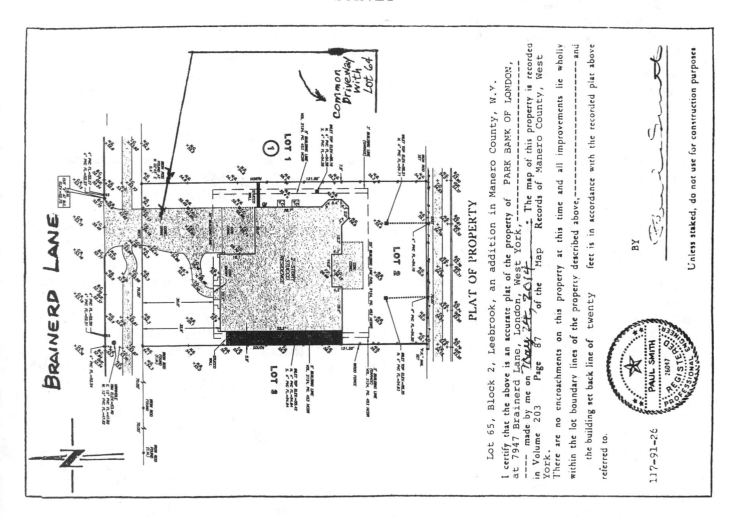

F. NOTES AND QUESTIONS ON FINANCING AND OTHER CONTINGENCIES

1. THE LOAN COMMITMENT. The commitment is a contract to fund the loan (although its generality may make contractual enforcement impractical). In some States, lenders frequently give verbal commitments. This practice is more common in states in which attorneys are not extensively involved.

2. THE GOOD FAITH ESTIMATE OF SETTLEMENT CHARGES; "RESPA." The Real Estate Settlement Procedures Act ("RESPA") is a federal statute imposing disclosure and other requirements upon real estate lenders. In particular, RESPA requires that the lender give the borrower a "good faith estimate" of the charges related to financing that will be incurred at closing. As implemented by regulations of the Department of Housing and Urban Development, RESPA also requires the lender to furnish the borrower a booklet promulgated by HUD explaining settlement costs and to furnish disclosures in a certain form at closing (see Chapter 6).

3. THE "COMMITMENT FEE," "ORIGINATION FEE," "DISCOUNT," ETC. The commitment requires the lender to produce funds when required by the borrower, irrespective of then-market conditions. Thus, the commitment fee is analogous to a fee for an option. The loan origination fee is a charge for efforts in funding the loan. Loan discount is prepaid interest. The meaning of these terms varies with the lender, and items denominated as fees may actually reflect the compensation the lender (or the marketplace) demands. Indeed, both lenders and borrowers often talk about these sums generically as "points." The careful borrower inquires about the components of the "points," for several reasons. They may be negotiable, and if they are really interest payments, they may be tax deductible.

4. USURY QUESTIONS. Note the lender's tendency to charge the borrower with each discrete cost attributable to his borrowing, rather than to charge a lump sum for loan processing. This tendency may have originated in lenders' concerns about usury laws. For many types of loans there are strictly defined maximum interest rates. But true costs of processing the loan may not be included in the interest. Particularly when market rates approach usury limits, lenders' attorneys face difficult questions in advising whether a given charge, such as a "loan origination fee," can validly be imposed—or whether it will be deemed interest by the law and thus cause the rate to be usurious. Lack of intent to charge usurious interest is not a defense, and penalties are often draconian. Thus real estate lawyers must be familiar with usury laws.

5. FEDERAL PRE-EMPTION OF STATE USURY LAWS. In the residential loan field, federal law pre-empts state usury limits (although States were able to re-enact their usury laws under certain conditions, most did not). Thus, mortgage lenders today need not ordinarily comply with usury limits, and the market is the principal regulator of residential interest rates. These federal laws were adopted in response to the unavailability of residential mortgage funds at rates complying with unduly restrictive state usury laws.

6. THE ENGINEERING REPORT. Why is the engineering inspection report so carefully hedged? (Hint: might the inspecting engineer incur liability for a report that is inadvertently misleading or inaccurate?) Notice the relationship of this report to the transaction: the "Property Condition Addendum" to the Earnest Money Contract gives buyer the right to make inspections and obligates seller to repair. At closing, as we shall see in Chapter 6, the items in the engineering report will be made the subject of further negotiations.

7. OTHER INSPECTIONS. In accordance with the lender's requirement, buyer obtained a certificate that the property was not in a defined flood hazard area (note that the earnest money contract makes no mention of this concern. It is interesting to speculate concerning seller's obligations if the residence were in such an area). Buyer also obtained a satisfactory termite inspection report and foundation inspection report.

CHAPTER FOUR

PREPARING THE "CORE" TRANSFER DOCUMENTS—THE NOTE, DEED AND MORTGAGE INSTRUMENTS

A note, a deed and a security instrument (a mortgage or deed of trust) are the core documents in almost all real estate transfers financed by lenders. In this transaction, the lender's attorney prepared all of the documents. Practice in this regard varies from State to State. The security instrument, in this case, was in a form called a "deed of trust," but the materials below will show you the "straight" mortgage as well.

A. PRELIMINARY NOTE: SORTING OUT THE PARTIES AND THE INSTRUMENTS; COMPARING THE "STRAIGHT" MORTGAGE WITH THE "DEED OF TRUST"

"MORTGAGE STATES" AND "DEED OF TRUST STATES." In some States, the use of a "deed of trust" or "trust deed mortgage" is common. Both the "straight" mortgage and the deed of trust serve the same purpose: to enable the lender to procure the sale of the security upon default by the borrower. But there is a difference. A mortgage is a two-party transaction between the lender and the borrower, which may or may not permit the lender to sell the property without judicial intervention. A deed of trust, on the other hand, is a three-party transaction in which the buyer conveys title in trust to a trustee for the benefit of the lender, and the trustee has the power of private sale upon default.

In some States, mortgages are customary; in other States, the deed of trust is the common method. Despite the distinction, there is not much practical difference between a mortgage containing a power of private sale and a deed of trust; the main difference is in mortgages without the power of private sale, under which the lender must obtain a court order decreeing a judicial sale.

UNDERSTANDING THE CORE DOCUMENTS. The core documents in a deed-of-trust State might be summarized this way:

1. THE DEED: The SELLER executes the DEED, which conveys title to the BUYER.
2. THE NOTE: The BUYER executes the NOTE, which is payable to the LENDER, in consideration of the loaned funds.
3. THE DEED OF TRUST: The BUYER (who is also the borrower) executes the DEED OF TRUST to the TRUSTEE, who has the power of private sale for the benefit of the LENDER.

In mortgage States, the documents are similar, except that there is no trustee—the mortgage is executed by the buyer to the lender directly. If it does not provide a power of private sale, the mortgage is enforceable only by court order.

A WARNING: Students sometimes have difficulty following a transaction that includes a deed of trust. The conveyance to the trustee is the step that causes confusion. Remember, the transfer to the trustee is done solely for the purpose of securing the loan: the trustee's main function is to exercise the power of private sale upon default.

B. THE DEED

GENERAL
WARRANTY DEED

Location & *Salutation*	THE STATE OF WEST YORK COUNTY OF MANERO } KNOW ALL PERSONS BY THESE PRESENTS:

Grantor
Identification

That PARK BANK OF LONDON, a banking corporation, Grantor

of the County of Manero and State of West York, for and in

consideration of the sum of Ten and no/100------------------------------

Consideration

--- ($10.00) DOLLARS

and other valuable consideration to the undersigned paid by the grantee s herein named, the receipt of

which is hereby acknowledged,

Granting
Clause

have GRANTED, SOLD AND CONVEYED, and by these presents do GRANT, SELL AND CONVEY unto
EDGAR E. PYNES, a baron sole, and ANDREW B. PYNES,

Grantee
Identification

of the County of Manero and State of West York , all of

the following described real property in Manero County, West York, to-wit:

Lot Sixty-Five (65), Block Two (2), of LEEBROOK
TOWN HOUSE SUBDIVISION, an addition to the City
of London, Manero County, West York, as per the
map or plat thereof, recorded in Volume 203,
Page 87 of the Map Records of Manero County,
West York,

Property
Description

Habendum
Clause

TO HAVE AND TO HOLD the above described premises, together with all and singular the rights and

appurtenances thereto in anywise belonging, unto the said grantee s, their heirs and assigns

forever; and it does hereby bind its successors and assigns to

Warranty
Clause

WARRANT AND FOREVER DEFEND all and singular the said premises unto the said grantee s, their

heirs and assigns, against every person whomsoever lawfully claiming or to claim the same or any part thereof.

This conveyance is made and accepted subject to any
and all conditions, restrictions and encumbrances of
record, relating to the hereinabove described property.

Exceptions or
Reservations

Current real estate taxes affecting the above
described property have been prorated between the parties and payment of same is hereby assumed by Grantees.

EXECUTED this 30th day of June , A.D. 2014.

Execution

PARK BANK OF LONDON

by: *Michael E. Way*

Vice President

28

THE STATE OF WEST YORK }
COUNTY OF MANERO }

Before me, the undersigned authority, on this day personally appeared MICHAEL E. WAY

Vice President of PARK BANK OF LONDON

a corporation, known to me to be the person whose name is subscribed to the foregoing instrument, and acknowledged to me that he executed the same for the purposes and consideration therein expressed, in the capacity therein stated and as the act and deed of said corporation.

Given under my hand and seal of office on this the ___30th___ day of ___June___, A.D. 2014.

Andrew A. Doitsch

Notary Public in and for Manero County, W.Y.

C. NOTES AND QUESTIONS ON THE DEED

1. **ELEMENTS OF THE DEED.** The elements are identified on the instrument by their traditional names, in italics. These designations were added for this book and are not part of the instrument.

2. **THE DEED IS A CONVEYANCE.** This instrument differs from an installment sale or "contract for deed" in that it is a present conveyance of title.

3. **THE GENERAL WARRANTY DEED DISTINGUISHED FROM OTHER CONVEYANCING INSTRUMENTS.** This instrument is a "general warranty deed." It differs from a "special warranty deed," which warrants the title only "by, through or under [the grantor]," meaning that the grantor is liable only for defects in the chain of title under him; and from the "quit-claim" (which conveys only such right, title and interest" as the grantor holds, so that one can give a perfectly lawful quit-claim deed to the Brooklyn Bridge—or to the Moon, for that matter). The general warranty deed creates liability in the grantor not only for defects in title attributable to him, but for defects in the title chain preceding him.

4. **EXCEPTIONS TO TITLE.** What happens if the deed describes the property without mentioning exceptions to title, such as deed restrictions, liens, or easements? In that case, the grantor owns only part of the pie, but he has purported to convey the entire pie—and has warranted the conveyance of the entire pie. It is easy to forget certain title exceptions (prorated taxes, which can constitute an encumbrance, are an example.) In this case, the deed simply excepts all encumbrances that are "of record." This convention is easier, all inclusive, and shorter (compare the long list in the Title Policy, below). A careful buyer might insist that each exception be individually specified.

5. **ACKNOWLEDGEMENT AND RECORDING.** The grantor "acknowledges" to a notary public that the instrument is what it purports to be and was in fact given for the consideration expressed in it. This clause may seem an archaic formalism, but it is necessary in many jurisdictions if the instrument is to be recorded.

6. **CORPORATE RESOLUTION.** A careful grantee might insist upon evidence of an authorizing resolution when the grantor is not an individual. The concern is that, even if Park Bank owns what the deed purports to convey, the deed will not convey it if the officer lacks authority to execute it.

7. **ESTATES IN LAND.** What estate is conveyed by this instrument? (The answer, of course, is a fee simple; why?) Of course, it is only a fee simple in what the grantor owned, i.e., the land less the exceptions to title.

8. **THE LAW OF MARITAL PROPERTY.** The deed recites that it is a conveyance to Edgar Pynes as "a baron sole," or single man. Such recitals may have significant importance for the interest received in community property States. For example, Andrew's (the father's) interest is presumed community if he is married, but in some States a recital could reverse the presumption.

9. **THE RESERVATION IN THE DEED OF AN EXPRESS VENDOR'S LIEN.** The deed in the real transaction was more complex than the one above, because the lender insisted upon the express reservation of a "vendor's lien" in the deed and the assignment of that lien to the lender. A vendor's lien is a purchase money security interest, arising because of a sale and securing a debt.

Therefore, the real deed contained an explanation of the consideration, describing the Note and stating that it was given in exchange for payment of $40,350 to the Grantor by the lender. After the warranty clause, the deed further contained the following language, by which the Grantor reserved the vendor's lien and assigned it to the lender:

But it is expressly agreed that the VENDOR'S LIEN, as well as the Superior Title in and to the above described premises, is retained against the above described property, premises and improvements until the above described note and all interest thereon are fully paid according to the face, tenor, effect and reading thereof, when this Deed shall become absolute.

The aforesaid Note represents a portion of the purchase price hereof and is payable directly to the Mortgagee, who has advanced money to the Grantors at the request of the Grantee, and in consideration thereof the Grantors do hereby sell, transfer and assign unto the Mortgagee, its successors and assigns, the Vendor's Lien and Superior Title herein retained against the above-described property and premises to secure payment of said Note, hereby fully and completely subrogating said Mortgagee, its successors and assigns, to all rights, titles, equities and interests in and to said Note, and all liens against said property securing payment thereof as if said Note were payable to Grantors and assigned to Mortgagee without recourse.

* * *

Actually, a vendor's lien arises in most states, by implication, whether it is expressly provided for or not. Why then incorporate it expressly in the deed? (Hint: if it isn't written, the vendor's lien can't be recorded, and if it isn't recorded, might it be effectively lost? There have been malpractice cases against attorneys for failing to express and record vendor's liens!) Also, why worry about the vendor's lien when there is a separate security instrument—the mortgage or deed of trust? (Hint: Is it conceivable that that instrument might somehow prove unenforceable? The vendor's lien is an extra safety belt, in case it does.)

D. THE NOTE (OR "PROMISSORY" NOTE)

NOTE ON THE SECONDARY MORTGAGE MARKET: FANNIE MAE AND HER FRIENDS

THE SECONDARY MORTGAGE MARKET. It is common for a Note secured by real estate to be sold by the original lender to an assignee, who succeeds to the right to obtain payments. Some mortgage companies exist primarily to originate loans that are then sold to others. Through this device, called the secondary mortgage market, capital flows from those lenders who have it to those who have customers to serve. (Incidentally, the borrower may never know of the sale, because the secondary mortgage buyer often employs the original lender to collect payments, called "servicing" the loan.)

FANNIE MAE, GINNIE MAE, AND FREDDIE MAC. In 1938, Congress established the Federal National Mortgage Association—which, because of its initials, "FNMA," has almost universally come to be called "Fannie Mae." The purpose of Fannie Mae is to create a national market in home mortgages, so that capital for home ownership will flow from parts of the country where it is in greatest supply to those where it is in greatest demand; and, further, it is Fannie Mae's purpose to make funds for home mortgages more plentiful by facilitating investment and smoothing fluctuations in the market. In 1968, Fannie Mae was restructured as a private corporation, and the Government National Mortgage Association ("Ginnie Mae") was created to support subsidy projects. Finally, in 1970, the Federal Home Loan Mortgage Corporation ("Freddie Mac") was established to perform functions analogous to those performed by Fannie Mae. Because of custom and regulatory differences, the majority of sales to Freddie Mac are by savings and loan associations and most sales to Fannie Mae are by institutions other than S& L's.

UNIFORM NATIONAL PROVISIONS. The national market has led to the promulgation by FNMA and FHLMC of instruments with uniform national provisions. The Note in this case is an example, as are the Mortgage, Deed of Trust, and Riders depicted below. These instruments are designed for sale on the national market, probably to Freddie Mac.

THE PROMISSORY NOTE
(EXCERPTS; DO NOT USE FOR DRAFTING)

INTEREST-ONLY PERIOD ADJUSTABLE RATE NOTE
(One-Year LIBOR Index – Rate Caps)

THIS NOTE CONTAINS PROVISIONS ALLOWING FOR A CHANGE IN MY FIXED INTEREST RATE TO AN ADJUSTABLE INTEREST RATE AND FOR CHANGES IN MY MONTHLY PAYMENT. THIS NOTE LIMITS THE AMOUNT MY ADJUSTABLE INTEREST RATE CAN CHANGE AT ANY ONE TIME AND THE MAXIMUM RATE I MUST PAY.

LONDON, WEST YORK   JUNE 30, 2014 [City/State]
7947 BRAINERD LANE, LONDON, WEST YORK 77040 [Property Address]

1. BORROWER'S PROMISE TO PAY

In return for a loan that I have received, I promise to pay U.S. $ 600,000 (this amount is called "Principal"), plus interest, to the order of Lender. Lender is HUNTINGTON SAVINGS ASSOCIATION, NA. I will make all payments under this Note in the form of cash, check or money order.

I understand that Lender may transfer this Note. Lender or anyone who takes this Note by transfer and who is entitled to receive payments under this Note is called the "Note Holder."

2. INTEREST

Interest will be charged on unpaid principal until the full amount of Principal has been paid. I will pay interest at a yearly rate of 4.250 %. The interest rate I will pay may change in accordance with Section 4 of this Note. * * *

3. PAYMENTS

(A) Time and Place of Payments

I will make a payment on the first day of every month, beginning on AUGUST 1, 2014. Before the First Principal and Interest Payment Due Date as described in Section 4 of this Note, my payment will consist only of the interest due on the unpaid principal balance of this Note. Thereafter, I will pay principal and interest by making a payment every month as provided below.

I will make my monthly payments of principal and interest beginning on the First Principal and Interest Payment Due Date as described in Section 4 of this Note. I will make these payments every month until I have paid all of the principal and interest and any other charges described below that I may owe under this Note. Each monthly payment will be applied as of its scheduled due date, and if the payment includes both principal and interest, it will be applied to interest before Principal. If, on SEPTEMBER1, 2044, I still owe amounts under this Note, I will pay those amounts in full on that date, which is called the "Maturity Date."

I will make my monthly payments at PO Box 11628, St. Petersburg FL 33733 or at a different place if required by the Note Holder.

(B) Amount of My Initial Monthly Payments

My monthly payment will be in the amount of U.S. $ 2125.00 before the First Principal and Interest Payment Due Date, and thereafter will be in an amount sufficient to repay the principal and interest at the rate determined as described in Section 4 of this Note in substantially equal installments by the Maturity Date. The Note Holder will notify me prior to the date of change in monthly payment.

(C) Monthly Payment Changes

Changes in my monthly payment will reflect changes in the unpaid principal of my loan and in the interest rate that I must pay. The Note Holder will determine my new interest rate and the changed amount of my monthly payment in accordance with Section 4 or 5 of this Note.

4. ADJUSTABLE INTEREST RATE AND MONTHLY PAYMENT CHANGES

(A) Change Dates

The initial fixed interest rate I will pay will change to an adjustable interest rate on the first day of _April, 2020, and the adjustable interest rate I will pay may change on that day every 12th month thereafter. The date on which my initial fixed interest rate changes to an adjustable interest rate, and each date on which my adjustable interest rate could change, is called a "Change Date."

(B) The Index

Beginning with the first Change Date, my adjustable interest rate will be based on an Index. The "Index" is the average of interbank offered rates for one-year U.S. dollar-denominated deposits in the London market ("LIBOR"), as published in *The Wall Street Journal*. The most recent Index figure available as of the date 45 days before each Change Date is called the "Current Index."

If the Index is no longer available, the Note Holder will choose a new index that is based upon comparable information. The Note Holder will give me notice of this choice.

(C) Calculation of Changes

Before each Change Date, the Note Holder will calculate my new interest rate by adding _2.00 percentage points (2.00%) to the Current Index. The Note Holder will then round the result of this addition to the nearest one-eighth of one percentage point (0.125%). Subject to the limits stated in Section 4(D) below, this rounded amount will be my new interest rate until the next Change Date.

The Note Holder will then determine the amount of the monthly payment that would be sufficient to repay the unpaid principal that I am expected to owe at the Change Date in full on the Maturity Date at my new interest rate in substantially equal payments. The result of this calculation will be the new amount of my monthly payment.

(D) Limits on Interest Rate Changes

The interest rate I am required to pay at the first Change Date will not be greater than _6.250 % or less than _2.875 %. Thereafter, my adjustable interest rate will never be increased or decreased on any single Change Date by more than two percentage points from the rate of interest I have been paying for the preceding 12 months. My interest rate will never be greater than _9.250 %.

(E) Effective Date of Changes

My new interest rate will become effective on each Change Date. I will pay the amount of my new monthly payment beginning on the first monthly payment date after the Change Date until the amount of my monthly payment changes again.

(F) Notice of Changes

Before the effective date of any change in my interest rate and/or monthly payment, the Note Holder will deliver or mail to me a notice of such change. * * *

5. BORROWER'S RIGHT TO PREPAY

I have the right to make payments of Principal at any time before they are due. A payment of Principal only is known as a "Prepayment." When I make a Prepayment, I will tell the Note Holder in writing that I am doing so. * * *

6. LOAN CHARGES

If a law, which applies to this loan and which sets maximum loan charges, is finally interpreted so that the interest or other loan charges collected or to be collected in connection with this loan exceed the permitted limits, then: (a) any such loan charge shall be reduced by the amount necessary to reduce the charge to the permitted limit; and (b) any sums already collected from me that exceeded permitted limits will be refunded to me. * * *

7. BORROWER'S FAILURE TO PAY AS REQUIRED

(A) Late Charges for Overdue Payments

If the Note Holder has not received the full amount of any monthly payment by the end of _fifteen calendar days after the date it is due, I will pay a late charge to the Note Holder. The amount of the charge will be _5.00 % of my overdue payment of interest, during the period when my payment is interest only, and of principal and interest thereafter. I will pay this late charge promptly but only once on each late payment.

(B) Default

If I do not pay the full amount of each monthly payment on the date it is due, I will be in default.

(C) Notice of Default

If I am in default, the Note Holder may send me a written notice telling me that if I do not pay the overdue amount by a certain date, the Note Holder may require me to pay immediately the full amount of Principal that has not been paid and all the interest that I owe on that amount. That date must be at least 30 days after the date on which the notice is mailed to me or delivered by other means.

(D) No Waiver By Note Holder

Even if, at a time when I am in default, the Note Holder does not require me to pay immediately in full as described above, the Note Holder will still have the right to do so if I am in default at a later time.

(E) Payment of Note Holder's Costs and Expenses

If the Note Holder has required me to pay immediately in full as described above, the Note Holder will have the right to be paid back by me for all of its costs and expenses in enforcing this Note to the extent not prohibited by applicable law. Those expenses include, for example, reasonable attorneys' fees.

8. GIVING OF NOTICES

Unless applicable law requires a different method, any notice that must be given to me under this Note will be given by delivering it or by mailing it by first class mail to me at the Property Address above or at a different address if I give the Note Holder a notice of my different address. * * *

9. OBLIGATIONS OF PERSONS UNDER THIS NOTE

If more than one person signs this Note, each person is fully and personally obligated to keep all of the promises made in this Note, including the promise to pay the full amount owed. Any person who is a guarantor, surety or endorser of this Note is also obligated to do these things. Any person who takes over these obligations, including the obligations of a guarantor, surety or endorser of this Note, is also obligated to keep all of the promises made in this Note. The Note Holder may enforce its rights under this Note against each person individually or against all of us together. This means that any one of us may be required to pay all of the amounts owed under this Note.

10. WAIVERS

I and any other person who has obligations under this Note waive the rights of Presentment and Notice of Dishonor. "Presentment" means the right to require the Note Holder to demand payment of amounts due. "Notice of Dishonor" means the right to require the Note Holder to give notice to other persons that amounts due have not been paid.

11. UNIFORM SECURED NOTE

This Note is a uniform instrument with limited variations in some jurisdictions. In addition to the protections given to the Note Holder under this Note, a Mortgage, Deed of Trust, or Security Deed (the "Security Instrument"), dated the same date as this Note, protects the Note Holder from possible losses that might result if I do not keep the promises that I make in this Note. That Security Instrument describes how and under what conditions I may be required to make immediate payment in full of all amounts I owe under this Note. * * *

WITNESS THE HAND(S) AND SEAL(S) OF THE UNDERSIGNED.

Elgar E. Pynes (Seal)
-Borrower

Ardeus E. Pynes (Seal)
-Borrower

[Sign Original Only]

MULTISTATE INTEREST-ONLY PERIOD ADJUSTABLE RATE NOTE—ONE-YEAR LIBOR INDEX— Form 3530 11/01 (rev. 9/06) Single Family—Fannie Mae Uniform Instrument

E. NOTES AND QUESTIONS ON THE PROMISSORY NOTE

1. NEGOTIABLE INSTRUMENT. The note is a negotiable instrument, providing the holder with certain benefits and making it more readily transferable. (This one, in fact, is likely to be sold on the "secondary mortgage market," which is discussed above.) You can learn more about negotiable instruments in a course in Commercial Law.

2. THE ADJUSTABLE RATE FEATURE AND THE CAP. Notice that the Note contains the adjustable rate feature discussed in the preceding chapter. The index to which it ties the interest rate is a figure periodically published by the Federal Reserve Board, expressing the average interest rate on "T-bills" (United States Treasury securities). This index is chosen because it is a relatively accurate reflection of the market for loaned funds and for its likelihood of consistent definition throughout the loan. The adjustment takes place in annual increments, on the first day of the month following each anniversary of the execution of the note. Notice also that the adjustment is "capped." There are actually two different caps: a cap limiting each annual jump to two percent, and a cap expressing the highest rate that can ever be attained.

3. OTHER BORROWER PROTECTIONS: "LIMITED PAYMENTS" AND EXTENDING THE LOAN. In addition to caps, some modern Notes allow the borrower to limit his payments and extend the maturity date for the loan when adjustments would exceed a given amount.

4. THE PREPAYMENT FEATURE. A note may either contain a prepayment penalty, or it may be prepayable without penalty (as this one is). What is the rationale underlying a penalty? It is that the lender is in the business of lending funds at interest and has a right to rely upon the income stream for which it contracted. The penalty is compensation to the lender for, in effect, rearranging its affairs because of the borrower's decision to prepay or, perhaps, for the loss of a favorable interest rate or of any interest for the period during which it seeks another borrower for the funds prepaid. The presence or absence of a prepayment feature is a point of negotiation between borrower and lender.

5. DEFAULT AND ACCELERATION. The note provides means for the lender to "accelerate" upon default, or to declare the balance due and payable. Without this clause, the noteholder would be reduced to suing each month for each payment as it became due. The acceleration provision is relatively favorable to the borrower: it requires a written notice first, after which the lender cannot accelerate for thirty days (during which the borrower may cure the default). Even then, acceleration is not automatic but depends upon a declaration by the lender requiring payment. (A harsher note might not provide for notice or might make acceleration effective without separate declaration.) Some states regulate by statute the manner in which lenders may exercise their rights under the clause, and some allow the default borrower to avoid the acceleration if he cures his default within a specified period of time. It is also possible that the buyer could avoid the acceleration by seeking relief in bankruptcy.

6. ANTI-WAIVER PROVISIONS. What happens if the borrower makes a payment two months late and the lender deposits his check? Does the lender thereby waive its right to accelerate; and has it inadvertently acceded to a new payment schedule by which each succeeding payment will be two months late? The instrument expressly negates that effect. However, the lender cannot effectively prevent all future modifications or waivers, and the harsh nature of the remedy of acceleration may make it difficult for the lender to make its position stand in court.

7. PERSONAL LIABILITY. The borrowers remain personally liable on the note even if they sell the property (unless the lender releases them). Why does the lender want this provision? Notice that the liability is joint and several; upon default, for example, the lender could sue the father alone and recover the entire amount from him. This arrangement differs from one in which the father might serve as a guarantor, which (for reasons beyond the scope of this book) might make collecting from him more difficult as a practical matter.

F. THE SECURITY INSTRUMENT: MORTGAGE OR DEED OF TRUST

"MORTGAGE" OR "DEED OF TRUST?" A LOOK AT BOTH KINDS OF INSTRUMENTS

THIS BOOK IS DESIGNED TO BE USED IN BOTH MORTGAGE AND DEED OF TRUST STATES, AND THEREFORE BOTH KINDS OF INSTRUMENTS ARE REPRODUCED HERE. The mortgage is adapted from a form promulgated by FNMA for Illinois. The deed of trust is adapted from Fannie Mae's Texas form. Actually, these forms are similar to those used, respectively, in other mortgage States (such as New York, for example) or other deed of trust States (California, for example). They are composed in large part of uniform nationwide provisions (the "uniform covenants") , supplemented by relatively few "non-uniform" covenants for the particular State.

You can obtain a fair appreciation of the appearance of the appropriate document in your State by considering either the mortgage or the deed of trust below, together with the uniform covenants (which happen to be attached to the deed of trust here).

FIRST ALTERNATIVE FORM: THE "STRAIGHT MORTGAGE"

MORTGAGE

DEFINITIONS [The document begins with definitions, including the identities of the borrower and lender, that are analogous to those in the next alternative form].

TRANSFER OF RIGHTS IN THE PROPERTY
This Security Instrument secures to Lender: (i) the repayment of the Loan, and all renewals, extensions and modifications of the Note; and (ii) the performance of Borrower's covenants and agreements under this Security Instrument and the Note.   For this purpose, Borrower does hereby mortgage, grant and convey to Lender and Lender's successors and assigns the following described property located in the <u>City of London, Manero County,West York,</u>

<u>Lot 65, Block 2, Leebrook Town House Subdivision, an addition to the City of London, Manero County, West York,</u>
which currently has the address of <u>7947 Brainerd Lane, London, West York 77040,</u>

TOGETHER WITH all the improvements now or hereafter erected on the property, and all easements, appurtenances, and fixtures now or hereafter a part of the property. All replacements and additions shall also be covered by this Security Instrument. All of the foregoing is referred to in this Security Instrument as the "Property."

[Notice that the conveyance is not a conveyance of the entire bundle of rights in the property and, specifically, does not convey "ownership" of the property; it conveys only a mortgage, or in other words a security interest securing the debt reflected by the loan.]
[In the next paragraphs, this instrument follows the next instrument (the "Deed of Trust). It concludes with paragraphs unique to the law of the particular state].

SECOND ALTERNATIVE MORTGAGE FORM: DEED OF TRUST
(EXCERPTS ONLY; DO NOT USE FOR DRAFTING)

DEED OF TRUST

DEFINITIONS * * * **(A) "Security Instrument"** means this document, which is dated March 14, 20214, together with all Riders to this document.

(B) "Borrower" is <u>EDGAR E. PYNES AND ANDREW B. PYNES.</u> Borrower is the grantor under this Security Instrument.

(C) "Lender" is <u>HUNTINGTON SAVINGS BANK NA.</u> Lender is a <u>Federal Savings Bank</u> organized and existing under the laws of Florida. * * * Lender is the beneficiary under this Security Instrument.

(D) "Trustee" is <u>ALBERT R. BALLARD [the attorney who drafted this instrument].</u> * * *

(E) "Note" means the promissory note signed by Borrower and dated <u>MARCH 14, 2014.</u> The Note states that Borrower owes Lender <u>SIX HUNDRED THOUSAND</u> Dollars (U.S. $ <u>600,000.00</u>) plus interest. Borrower has promised to pay this debt in regular Periodic Payments * * *

TRANSFER OF RIGHTS IN THE PROPERTY

This Security Instrument secures to Lender: (i) the repayment of the Loan, and all renewals, extensions and modifications of the Note; and (ii) the performance of Borrower's covenants and agreements under this Security Instrument and the Note. For this purpose, Borrower irrevocably grants and conveys to Trustee, in trust, with power of sale, the following described property located in the <u>State</u> of <u>West York</u>:

> <u>Lot 65, Block 2, Leebrook Town House Subdivision, an addition to the city of London, Manero County, West York</u>

which currently has the address of <u>7947 Brainerd Lane, London, West York 77040,</u>

TOGETHER WITH all the improvements now or hereafter erected on the property, and all easements, appurtenances, and fixtures now or hereafter a part of the property. All replacements and additions shall also be covered by this Security Instrument. All of the foregoing is referred to in this Security Instrument as the "Property."

BORROWER COVENANTS that Borrower is lawfully seised of the estate hereby conveyed and has the right to grant and convey the Property and that the Property is unencumbered, except for encumbrances of record. Borrower warrants and will defend generally the title to the Property against all claims and demands, subject to any encumbrances of record.

THIS SECURITY INSTRUMENT combines uniform covenants for national use and non-uniform covenants with limited variations by jurisdiction to constitute a uniform security instrument covering real property.

UNIFORM COVENANTS. Borrower and Lender covenant and agree as follows:

1. Payment of Principal, Interest, Escrow Items, Prepayment Charges, and Late Charges. Borrower shall pay when due the principal of, and interest on, the debt evidenced by the Note and any prepayment charges and late charges due under the Note. Borrower shall also pay funds for Escrow Items pursuant to Section 3. * * *

3. Funds for Escrow Items. Borrower shall pay to Lender on the day Periodic Payments are due under the Note, until the Note is paid in full, a sum (the "Funds") to provide for payment of amounts due for: (a) taxes and assessments and other items which can attain priority over this Security Instrument as a lien or encumbrance on the Property; (b) leasehold payments or ground rents on the Property, if any; (c) premiums for any and all insurance required by Lender under Section 5; and (d) Mortgage Insurance premiums, if any, or any sums payable by Borrower to Lender in lieu of the payment of Mortgage Insurance premiums in accordance with the provisions of Section 10. These items are called "Escrow Items." * * *

Lender shall give to Borrower, without charge, an annual accounting of the Funds as required by RESPA [which is a federal act applicable to some real estate transactions]. * * * Upon payment in full of all sums secured by this Security Instrument, Lender shall promptly refund to Borrower any Funds held by Lender.

4. Charges; Liens. Borrower shall pay all taxes, assessments, charges, fines, and impositions attributable to the Property which can attain priority over this Security Instrument, leasehold payments or ground rents on the Property, if any, and Community Association Dues, Fees, and Assessments, if any. To the extent that these items are Escrow Items, Borrower shall pay them in the manner provided in Section 3.

Borrower shall promptly discharge any lien which has priority over this Security Instrument * * *.

5. Property Insurance. Borrower shall keep the improvements now existing or hereafter erected on the Property insured against loss by fire, hazards included within the term "extended coverage," and any other hazards including, but not limited to, earthquakes and floods, for which Lender requires insurance. This insurance shall be maintained in the amounts (including deductible levels) and for the periods that Lender requires. * * * The insurance carrier providing the insurance shall be chosen by Borrower subject to Lender's right to disapprove Borrower's choice, which right shall not be exercised unreasonably. * * *

If Borrower fails to maintain any of the coverages described above, Lender may obtain insurance coverage, at Lender's option and Borrower's expense. * * * Borrower acknowledges that the cost of the insurance coverage so obtained might significantly exceed the cost of insurance that Borrower could have obtained. Any amounts disbursed by Lender under this Section 5 shall become additional debt of Borrower secured by this Security Instrument. * * *

All insurance policies required by Lender and renewals of such policies shall be subject to Lender's right to disapprove such policies, shall include a standard mortgage clause, and shall name Lender as mortgagee and/or as an additional loss payee. * * *

7. Preservation, Maintenance and Protection of the Property; Inspections. Borrower shall not destroy, damage or impair the Property, allow the Property to deteriorate or commit waste on the Property. Whether or not Borrower is residing in the Property, Borrower shall maintain the Property in order to prevent the Property from deteriorating or decreasing in value due to its condition. * * *

Lender or its agent may make reasonable entries upon and inspections of the Property. If it has reasonable cause, Lender may inspect the interior of the improvements * * *.

9. Protection of Lender's Interest in the Property and Rights Under this Security Instrument. If (a) Borrower fails to perform the covenants and agreements contained in this

Security Instrument, (b) there is a legal proceeding that might significantly affect Lender's interest in the Property and/or rights under this Security Instrument (such as a proceeding in bankruptcy, probate, for condemnation or forfeiture, for enforcement of a lien which may attain priority over this Security Instrument or to enforce laws or regulations), or (c) Borrower has abandoned the Property, then Lender may do and pay for whatever is reasonable or appropriate to protect Lender's interest in the Property and rights under this Security Instrument * * *.

10. Mortgage Insurance. If Lender required Mortgage Insurance as a condition of making the Loan, Borrower shall pay the premiums required to maintain the Mortgage Insurance in effect. * * *

Mortgage Insurance reimburses Lender (or any entity that purchases the Note) for certain losses it may incur if Borrower does not repay the Loan as agreed. Borrower is not a party to the Mortgage Insurance. * * *

12. Borrower Not Released; Forbearance By Lender Not a Waiver. Extension of the time for payment or modification of amortization of the sums secured by this Security Instrument granted by Lender to Borrower or any Successor in Interest of Borrower shall not operate to release the liability of Borrower or any Successors in Interest of Borrower. * * * Any forbearance by Lender in exercising any right or remedy including, without limitation, Lender's acceptance of payments from third persons, entities or Successors in Interest of Borrower or in amounts less than the amount then due, shall not be a waiver of or preclude the exercise of any right or remedy.

13. Joint and Several Liability; Co-signers; Successors and Assigns Bound. Borrower covenants and agrees that Borrower's obligations and liability shall be joint and several. * * *

14. Loan Charges. * * * If the Loan is subject to a law which sets maximum loan charges, and that law is finally interpreted so that the interest or other loan charges collected or to be collected in connection with the Loan exceed the permitted limits, then: (a) any such loan charge shall be reduced by the amount necessary to reduce the charge to the permitted limit; and (b) any sums already collected from Borrower which exceeded permitted limits will be refunded to Borrower. * * *

15. Notices. * * * Notice to any one Borrower shall constitute notice to all Borrowers unless Applicable Law expressly requires otherwise. The notice address shall be the Property Address unless Borrower has designated a substitute notice address by notice to Lender. * * * Any notice to Lender shall be given by delivering it or by mailing it by first class mail to Lender's address stated herein unless Lender has designated another address by notice to Borrower. * * *

16. Governing Law; Severability; Rules of Construction. This Security Instrument shall be governed by federal law and the law of the jurisdiction in which the Property is located. * * *

18. Transfer of the Property or a Beneficial Interest in Borrower. * * * If all or any part of the Property or any Interest in the Property is sold or transferred (or if Borrower is not a natural person and a beneficial interest in Borrower is sold or transferred) without Lender's prior written consent, Lender may require immediate payment in full of all sums secured by this Security Instrument. * * *

19. Borrower's Right to Reinstate After Acceleration. If Borrower meets certain conditions, Borrower shall have the right to have enforcement of this Security Instrument discontinued at any time prior to the earliest of: (a) five days before sale of the Property pursuant to any power of sale contained in this Security Instrument; (b) such other period as Applicable Law might specify for the termination of Borrower's right to reinstate; or (c) entry of a judgment enforcing this Security Instrument. Those conditions are that Borrower: (a) pays Lender all sums which then would be due under this Security Instrument and the Note as if no acceleration had occurred; (b) cures any default of any other covenants or agreements; (c) pays all expenses incurred in enforcing this Security Instrument * * *.

    20. Sale of Note; Change of Loan Servicer * * *. The Note or a partial interest in the Note (together with this Security Instrument) can be sold one or more times without prior notice to Borrower. A sale might result in a change in the entity (known as the "Loan Servicer") that collects Periodic Payments due under the Note and this Security Instrument and performs other mortgage loan servicing obligations under the Note, this Security Instrument, and Applicable Law. There also might be one or more changes of the Loan Servicer unrelated to a sale of the Note. * * *

    NON-UNIFORM COVENANTS. Borrower and Lender further covenant and agree as follows:

    22. Acceleration; Remedies. Lender shall give notice to Borrower prior to acceleration following Borrower's breach of any covenant or agreement in this Security Instrument (but not prior to acceleration under Section 18 unless Applicable Law provides otherwise). The notice shall specify: (a) the default; (b) the action required to cure the default; (c) a date, not less than 30 days from the date the notice is given to Borrower, by which the default must be cured; and (d) that failure to cure the default on or before the date specified in the notice will result in acceleration of the sums secured by this Security Instrument and sale of the Property. The notice shall further inform Borrower of the right to reinstate after acceleration and the right to bring a court action to assert the non-existence of a default or any other defense of Borrower to acceleration and sale. If the default is not cured on or before the date specified in the notice, Lender at its option may require immediate payment in full of all sums secured by this Security Instrument without further demand and may invoke the power of sale and any other remedies permitted by Applicable Law. Lender shall be entitled to collect all expenses incurred in pursuing the remedies provided in this Section 22, including, but not limited to, reasonable attorneys' fees and costs of title evidence. For the purposes of this Section 22, the term "Lender" includes any holder of the Note who is entitled to receive payments under the Note.

    If Lender invokes the power of sale, Lender or Trustee shall give notice of the time, place and terms of sale by posting and filing the notice at least 21 days prior to sale as provided by Applicable Law. Lender shall mail a copy of the notice to Borrower in the manner prescribed by Applicable Law. Sale shall be made at public vendue. The sale must begin at the time stated in the notice of sale or not later than three hours after that time and between the hours of 10 a.m. and 4 p.m. on the first Tuesday of the month. Borrower authorizes Trustee to sell the Property to the highest bidder for cash in one or more parcels and in any order Trustee determines. Lender or its designee may purchase the Property at any sale.

    Trustee shall deliver to the purchaser Trustee's deed conveying indefeasible title to the Property with covenants of general warranty from Borrower. Borrower covenants and agrees to defend generally the purchaser's title to the Property against all claims and demands. The recitals in the Trustee's deed shall be prima facie evidence of the truth of the statements made therein. Trustee shall apply the proceeds of the sale in the following order: (a) to all expenses

of the sale, including, but not limited to, reasonable Trustee's and attorneys' fees; (b) to all sums secured by this Security Instrument; and (c) any excess to the person or persons legally entitled***.

       23. Release. Upon payment of all sums secured by this Security Instrument, Lender shall provide a release of this Security Instrument to Borrower or Borrower's designated agent in accordance with Applicable Law. * * *

       24. Substitute Trustee; Trustee Liability. * * * Lender, at its option and with or without cause, may from time to time, by power of attorney or otherwise, remove or substitute any trustee, add one or more trustees, or appoint a successor trustee to any Trustee without the necessity of any formality other than a designation by Lender in writing. * * (

       Trustee shall not be liable if acting upon any notice, request, consent, demand, statement or other document believed by Trustee to be correct. Trustee shall not be liable for any act or omission unless such act or omission is willful. * * *

       BY SIGNING BELOW, Borrower accepts and agrees to the terms and covenants contained in this Security Instrument and in any Rider executed by Borrower and recorded with it. * * *

_____   *Edgar E. Pynes*   (Seal)
                                                                              Borrower

_____   *Andrew B. Pynes*   (Seal)
                                                                          - Borrower

_____ **[Space Below This Line For Acknowledgment]** _____
[Note that there must be acknowledgement for the document to be recorded. Accordingly, here there were acknowledgments by both borrowers.]

["**West York**"]--Single Family--**Fannie Mae/Freddie Mac UNIFORM INSTRUMENT**

NOTE: COMPARING THIS TRANSACTION WITH A BIGGER, COMMERCIAL SALE

      The Note, Deed and Mortgage (or Deed of Trust) embody the same concept whether the sale is small or large. Therefore, although it may surprise you, the core documents in a much bigger transaction are likely to be very similar to those reproduced above. Some provisions in the Note or Mortgage may reflect differences in the financing negotiations (such as additional security terms or absence of personal liability). More fundamental conceptual differences are likely to be reflected in the contract of purchase and sale, or in the ancillary documents and contingencies at closing.

G. NOTES AND QUESTIONS ON THE MORTGAGE (OR DEED OF TRUST)

1. THE UNIFORM COVENANTS. The above forms are written so that the beginning phraseology is particularized for each State, but the rest of each instrument is a set of "uniform covenants" that can be used nationwide.

2. THE JUDICIAL-SALE MORTGAGE. The Mortgage without power of private sale provides superior judicial protection to the borrower (at least, it does so on paper). The disadvantage of the requirement of judicial enforcement is that it results in significantly greater expense and delay to the lender faced with a truly defaulting borrower. This disadvantage is silently incorporated into the cost of the loan for all borrowers.

3. THE PRIVATE-SALE MORTGAGE; DEED OF TRUST. Remember how the deed of trust works: the borrower-buyer conveys to a trustee who has the power to sell the encumbered property upon default. Judicial process is not required. What if a borrower is faced with an oppressive or otherwise wrongful foreclosure? (The answer: foreclosure must be preceded by statutory notice periods. The standard practice in deed of trust States is for the borrower to bring an action to enjoin foreclosure. Wrongful foreclosure under a deed of trust is actionable in some jurisdictions in damages.) Thus the borrower is not deprived of judicial redress; the deed of trust simply shifts the necessity of going to court from lender to borrower. But this change is a significant one.

4. MAGNITUDE OF THE DELAY IN FORECLOSURE. Foreclosure law is exacting, and borrowers can obtain injunctions in a significant proportion of trust deed sales. See H. MORRIS, HOW TO STOP FORECLOSURE (1983) (advising that "The lender doesn't have much time to spend on your individual mortgage. But if you are in foreclosure you have the time to look for loopholes and mistakes"). In one major trust deed State (Texas), the average time from default to foreclosure is about six months. Houston Chronicle (reporting on various mortgages). But "in many [mortgage] States, foreclosure processes can take up to two years." Id. By considering a lender faced with even a small portion of loans that go two years without payment, one can appreciate the magnitude of the problem.

5. WHICH IS BETTER: MORTGAGE OR DEED OF TRUST? You should consider the advantages and disadvantages of each type of instrument.

6. EQUITY OF REDEMPTION. The borrower has the right to prevent foreclosure by paying after default, called the "equity of redemption." This right arises from decisional law and by statute; it varies from State to State. This instrument provides for a 30-day period after Notice before acceleration may take place.

7. ESCROW FOR TAXES AND INSURANCE. The borrower is required to pay taxes and insure the collateral. But since the lender cannot otherwise enforce this obligation, it is enforced by the requirement that the borrower pay an additional sum in his monthly payment to the lender, who then pays taxes and insurance premiums. The lender holds these funds in "escrow" (i.e., in a special purpose account, and as a kind of stakeholder); each year, payments for the escrow fund are raised or lowered according to the lender's estimate of the amount needed for the coming year. Sometimes lenders do not require such an escrow (or impound, as it is sometimes called) where the borrower has made a sizeable down payment. This matter may also be regulated by Statute.

8. MORTGAGE INSURANCE. In addition to hazard insurance, the instrument contemplates "mortgage insurance." Such insurance compensates the lender for inability to realize its indebtedness upon sale, as provided.

9. PHYSICAL INTEGRITY OF THE PROPERTY. Several covenants deal with the physical maintenance of the collateral. What if borrower tears down all internal walls, for instance? (He may have violated the covenant in paragraph 7 against deterioration, waste, or "substantial change"). There is coverage of casualty loss, condemnation, and other contingencies.

10. FORECLOSURE PROCEDURE. Foreclosure is governed by the law of the State, and it is also subject to the covenants contained in the mortgage instrument. In this case, paragraph 22 contains extensive specification of the procedure for foreclosure. Is detail a good idea? Not from the lender's point of

view, because each detail is an additional requirement that must be correctly met. Occasionally, it happens that a deed of trust is written so that it is impossible for foreclosure to comply both with the covenants in the instrument and with state law (e.g., state law provides that all sales shall be on the first Tuesday of the month, but the instrument provides that sale shall be on a Monday). In that event, the instrument cannot be non-judicially enforced, but judicial foreclosure would still be available.

11. TRUSTEE AND SUBSTITUTE TRUSTEE. Who is appointed as trustee? (If you were the lawyer drawing the instrument, who would you appoint? The answer: yourself, of course! Provided, that is, that the appointment is lawful, as it is in this jurisdiction.) In the average transaction, the likelihood is that the lawyer who drew the papers would name himself. Notice the provision for a substitute trustee. Without this clause, what would happen if the trustee died or was unable to act? The instrument could not then be non-judicially enforced.

12. PERSONAL LIABILITY AND "DEFICIENCY JUDGMENTS." Remember that the note creates personal liability in the borrower. If foreclosure fails to satisfy the debt, the lender may be able to obtain a deficiency judgment against the borrower. Many States have restricted this right, however, and some prohibit it after residential foreclosures. (What effect will such a prohibition have upon the cost and availability of credit? Is it wise?)

H. NOTES AND QUESTIONS ON THE DUE-ON-SALE CLAUSE

1. THE DUE-ON-SALE CLAUSE. Re-read paragraph 20 of the uniform covenants. Notice what it means. If the borrower sells the property and the lender has not previously consented to the sale, the lender may accelerate the balance of the note. Why does the lender want this apparently one-sided clause in the instrument? Or, to put the question in context, why does the federal government (which drafted this instrument) think lenders ought to have this right?

2. THE LENDER'S INTEREST IN CREDITWORTHY OBLIGORS. If the borrower sells to an uncreditworthy person, the lender may not be protected. The original borrower is still personally liable on the note but may not be easy to collect from.

3. THE LENDER'S INTEREST IN MAINTAINING A RELATIONSHIP BETWEEN THE RATE AT WHICH IT LENDS FUNDS AND THE RATE IT PAYS FOR DEPOSITS. Another reason the lender may want the due-on-sale clause is that it may want to raise the interest rate to the current market rate—particularly if it lent the money at a low fixed rate. Remember that this concern is an important one to lenders (and derivatively it is of concern to the entire economy).

4. THE DUE-ON-SALE CONTROVERSY AND ITS RESOLUTION. During the 1970's and early 1980's, there was extensive litigation concerning due-on-sale clauses. Some States held that raising the interest rate was not a lawful reason for exercise of the due-on-sale clause. The lender could only protect its right to a creditworthy obligor. Such holdings exacerbated an already severe squeeze for savings institutions, and they prompted passage of the Garn-St. Germain Depository Institutions Act of 1982. That Act of Congress invalidated state restrictions on due on sale clauses.

5. THE "GOLDEN RULE." An old Commercial Law adage holds that, "If you want to borrow my money, you'll first sign my documents." And real estate lawyers quote what they call the "Golden Rule:" "The lender has the Gold, and he Rules." The lender is about to pass a large sum of money into the hands of a stranger, with risk that conditions beyond the lender's control may cause it to suffer loss of all or part of the sum. The lender believes, accordingly, that it should be able to protect its position. The Garn-St. Germain Act may be evidence of Congress' persuasion that, at least to some extent, the Golden Rule is in the public interest.

I. RIDERS TO THE MORTGAGE INSTRUMENT

PLANNED UNIT DEVELOPMENT RIDER

THIS PLANNED UNIT DEVELOPMENT RIDER is made this 30TH day of JUNE , 2014 , and is incorporated into and shall be deemed to amend and supplement the Mortgage, Deed of Trust or Security Deed (the "Security Instrument") of the same date, given by the undersigned (the "Borrower") to secure Borrower's Note to

HUNTINGTON SAVINGS ASSOCIATION (the "Lender")

of the same date and covering the Property described in the Security Instrument and located at:

7947 BRAINERD LANE, LONDON, WEST YORK 77040
[Property Address]

The Property includes, but is not limited to, a parcel of land improved with a dwelling, together with other such parcels and certain common areas and facilities, as described in

DECLARATIONS AND COVENANTS

(the "Declaration"). The Property is a part of a planned unit development known as Leebrook Town House Subdivision, an addition to the City of London, Manero County, West York
[Name of Planned Unit Development]

(the "PUD"). The Property also includes Borrower's interest in the homeowners association or equivalent entity owning or managing the common areas and facilities of the PUD (the "Owners Association") and the uses, benefits and proceeds of Borrower's interest.

PUD COVENANTS. In addition to the covenants and agreements made in the Security Instrument, Borrower and Lender further covenant and agree as follows:

A. PUD Obligations. Borrower shall perform all of Borrower's obligations under the PUD's Constituent Documents. The "Constituent Documents" are the : (i) Declaration; (ii) articles of incorporation, trust instrument or any equivalent document which creates the Owners Association; and (iii) any by-laws or other rules or regulations of the Owners Association. Borrower shall promptly pay, when due, all dues and assessments imposed pursuant to the Constituent Documents.

* * *

[The instrument requires the borrower to refrain from participation in terminating the PUD without Lender's consent, to notify Lender of certain kinds of important changes in the PUD, and to take certain other steps to protect Lender's interest in the PUD. It also provides that if a blanket casualty insurance policy covering units in the PUD is in force in a form satisfactory to the Lender, a separate insurance policy is not necessary.]

F. Remedies. If Borrower does not pay PUD dues and assessments when due, then Lender may pay them. Any amounts disbursed by Lender under this paragraph F shall become additional debt of Borrower secured by the Security Instrument. Unless Borrower and Lender agree to other terms of payment, these amounts shall bear interest from the date of disbursement at the Note rate and shall be payable, with interest, upon notice from Lender to Borrower requesting payment.

BY SIGNING BELOW, Borrower accepts and agrees to the terms and provisions contained in this PUD Rider.

....(Seal)
—Borrower

Edgar E. Pynes ....(Seal)
EDGAR E. PYNES —Borrower

....(Seal)
—Borrower

Andrew B. Pynes ....(Seal)
ANDREW B. PYNES —Borrower

MULTISTATE PUD RIDER—Single Family—FNMA/FHLMC UNIFORM INSTRUMENT   Form 3150

ADJUSTABLE RATE RIDER
(Interest Rate Limits)

THIS ADJUSTABLE RATE RIDER is made this   30TH day of   JUNE   , 2014, and is incorporated into and shall be deemed to amend and supplement the Mortgage, Deed of Trust, or Deed to Secure Debt (the "Security Instrument") of the same date given by the undersigned (the "Borrower") to secure Borrower's Adjustable Rate Note to   HUNTINGTON SAVINGS ASSOCIATION
(the "Lender") of the same date (the "Note") and covering the property described in the Security Instrument and located at:

   7947 BRAINERD LANE, LONDON, WEST YORK 77040

[Property Address]

The Note contains provisions allowing for changes in the interest rate every 1 YEAR subject to the limits stated in the Note. If the interest rate increases, the Borrower's monthly payments will be higher. If the interest rate decreases, the Borrower's monthly payments will be lower.

ADDITIONAL COVENANTS. In addition to the covenants and agreements made in the Security Instrument, Borrower and Lender further covenant and agree as follows:

A. INTEREST RATE AND MONTHLY PAYMENT CHANGES

The Note provides for an initial interest rate of   4.25 %. Section 4 of the Note provides for changes in the interest rate and the monthly payments, as follows:

"4. INTEREST RATE AND MONTHLY PAYMENT CHANGES

* * *

[The Rider recapitulates the Adjustable Rate provisions of the Note. It also alters certain provisions of the uniform covenants to the Security Instrument (mortgage or deed of trust) to make them fit the Adjustable Rate features more appropriately. It concludes with the following:]

F. LOAN CHARGES

If the loan secured by the Security Instrument is subject to a law which sets maximum loan charges, and that law is finally interpreted so that the interest or other loan charges collected or to be collected in connection with the loan exceed permitted limits, then: (1) any such loan charge shall be reduced by the amount necessary to reduce the charge to the permitted limit; and (2) any sums already collected from Borrower which exceeded permitted limits will be refunded to Borrower. Lender may choose to make this refund by reducing the principal owed under the Note or by making a direct payment to Borrower. If a refund reduces principal, the reduction will be treated as a partial prepayment under the Note.

G. LEGISLATION

If, after the date hereof, enactment or expiration of applicable laws have the effect either of rendering the provisions of the Note, the Security Instrument or this Adjustable Rate Rider (other than this paragraph **G**) unenforceable according to their terms, or all or any part of the sums secured hereby uncollectable, as otherwise provided in the Security Instrument and this Adjustable Rate Rider, or of diminishing the value of Lender's security, then Lender, at Lender's option, may declare all sums secured by the Security Instrument to be immediately due and payable.

IN WITNESS WHEREOF, Borrower has executed this Adjustable Rate Rider.

....(Seal)
                                       —Borrower

Edgar E. Pynes
....(Seal)
                                       —Borrower
EDGAR E. PYNES

....(Seal)
                                       —Borrower

Andrew B. Pynes
....(Seal)
                                       —Borrower
ANDREW B. PYNES

44

J. NOTES AND QUESTIONS ON THE RIDERS TO THE MORTGAGE INSTRUMENT

1. THE PLANNED UNIT DEVELOPMENT RIDER. Why is the PUD Rider necessary? (Hint: The Declaration referred to in the Rider imposes maintenance assessments upon the owner of each lot, to maintain common areas. The Declaration undoubtedly creates a lien on the lot to secure the payment by each homeowner of his maintenance assessment. What might happen to this lender's security if the borrower failed to pay maintenance assessments, or for that matter if he failed to comply with other similarly enforceable provisions of the Declaration?)

2. THE ADJUSTABLE RATE RIDER: THE "USURY SAVINGS CLAUSE." Paragraph "G" of the Adjustable Rate Rider provides, in essence, that if any charge imposed by the Adjustable Rate Note proves to be usurious, it is automatically reduced to a lawful amount. Why might it be wise to include such a provision with the Adjustable Rate Note?

3. THE LENDER'S OWN "EXTRA PROTECTION" RIDER THAT SELF-DESTRUCTS UPON SALE TO FNMA OR FHLMC. These documents are drafted in a manner that is relatively liberal to borrowers, possibly because of the nature of FNMA and FHLMC. Lenders often add their own Riders, giving them greater authority to protect their security (e.g., defining acts of default as including bankruptcy or other conditions of the borrower, allowing acceleration in more instances, etc.). Such a Rider will generally contain language causing it to "self-destruct" (by providing that it shall be of no further force and effect if the note is assigned in the secondary mortgage market).

4. THE USE OF FORMS AND RIDERS AS DRAFTING DEVICES. These forms are set up for efficiency. Particulars are to be inserted in blanks at the beginning or end of each instrument (can you see why that is preferable to blanks sprinkled throughout, if rapid drafting is the object)? The addition of a Rider may be more efficient than making changes in the main instrument. In general, studies of document preparation by lawyers indicate that it often partakes of these techniques. Lawyers draft by cannibalizing existing forms to the fullest extent possible. Such "drafting" sometimes requires great skill if both efficiency and precision are to be achieved, even though the skill may not resemble what we normally think of as draftsmanship.

AN IMPORTANT NOTE ABOUT A CONSTANT WORRY: WHAT HAPPENS IF INTEREST RATES RISE?

INTEREST RATES MAKE *HUGE* DIFFERENCES. A significant increase in interest rates could double or triple the amount of the Borrower's monthly payment. Even an interest rate increase of less than a single point could make many hundreds of dollars' difference. Students sometimes have tendencies to think that a difference of one percent is "small." Don't assume that! It is not, and it can make an otherwise economical property uneconomical.

SO WHY THEN DOES THE BUYER HERE AGREE TO AN ADJUSTABLE RATE, WHICH CAN INCREASE? The Lender has the same concern. The Lender could find itself borrowing at a higher rate than it is taking in on this property. By using an adjustable rate, the Borrower induces the Lender to loan at an acceptable rate, now. For this particular loan, the rate is fixed for five years, and if inflation forces the rate up, the Borrower can hope for inflation in the Borrower's income, too. It's all about risk. If the Borrower wants to impose all the risk on the Lender, the Lender will insist on a higher initial rate.

THE "INTEREST ONLY" FEATURE IN THIS LOAN MEANS A LOWER PAYMENT FOR THE BORROWER. The Borrower in this case has obtained a significant benefit by obtaining an "interest only" loan. The Borrower's payment is of interest only, and no principal, so that the monthly payment is much lesser. This means that the Borrower does not buy any equity ownership with each payment. But the Borrower hopes for an increase in value, which is normally what happens to real estate; that would increase the Borrower's equity ownership in the property.

CHAPTER FIVE:

PREPARATION FOR TITLE ASSURANCE

INTRODUCTORY NOTE

One other major issue remained before closing: the status of the title. Did Park Bank really own the fee it had contracted to convey? If it did, was it free of prohibited encumbrances? If so, was the state of the record sufficiently unambiguous to comply with contract requirements, and if not, could it be cured?

These materials include excerpts from the chain of title all the way back to the patent from the sovereign. In a few jurisdictions, titles are routinely examined to this extent, although in most, a more limited search may be sufficient. There are also significant variations in the identity and role of the examiner.

A. EXCERPTS FROM THE CHAIN OF TITLE

NOTE ON THE GRANT (OR "PATENT") FROM THE SOVEREIGN: A STUDY IN HISTORY

One of the delightful aspects of title examination is that it sometimes makes colonial America, or Spanish land grants, or the great accords and treaties of international diplomacy come alive not just as history, but as a part of the present title chain.

West York, as it happens, was acquired by the United States through treaty (as were many States). It was once a part of Spain, then France, then Mexico—and it was while West York was part of Mexico that the land in question here was patented, through the authority of a Mexican jurisdiction known as the State of Coahuila.

CONFIRMATION PATENTS. Upon acquisition of land by treaty, titles were sometimes unclear. Typical practice was to set up a claims process, whereby either the United States or the State in which the land was located would confirm titles. This sovereign would cause the land to be surveyed if necessary, and it would issue a new patent, called a confirmation patent. Failure to obtain confirmation could result in loss of title (and adjudications to that effect, although rare today, still occur).

Of course, the patent was not limited to "Lot 65, Block 2 of the Leebrook Town House Subdivision." A land grant could be a big thing in those days, measured in "leagues" and "varas." A vara is a trifle less than 33 inches. The real grant here covered a square parcel with sides 1900 varas long, or roughly one square mile. For convenience, all measurements have been converted into feet here.

THE RICHARD ROWLES SURVEY. The patentee is one Richard Rowles, and the parcel is called the "Richard Rowles Survey." The document that follows is a facsimile of the pertinent parts of the actual patent, with most of the language taken verbatim from the document on file in the "real" Manero County Clerk's Office. The Richard Rowles Survey was about to begin a century and a quarter of transfers and divisions.

No 467, vol 46.   In the Name of the State of New York To all to whom these Presents shall come: Know Ye, I, J.S. Shoal, Governor of the State aforesaid, by virtue of the power vested in me by law, and in accordance with the laws of said State, in such case made and provided, do by these Presents grant unto Richard Rowles, his heirs or assigns forever ═══ Six hundred and forty (640) Acres of land, situated and described as follows. In Manero County, on the waters of White Oak Bayou, about 11½ miles North 58° W. from London, by virtue of Headright Cert. No 266 issued to said Rowles by the Court of Claims July 7th 1860, to-wit: BEGINNING at the S.W. cor. of Joseph Bays on the east line of A. Area at a stake, Thence east 5,225 feet and crossing a branch of White Oak Bayou at 3,355 feet to a stake in prairie, Thence south 5,225 feet crossing same branch at 572 feet to a stake for cor. Thence west 5,225 feet to a stake for S.W. cor. Thence North 5,225 feet along the east line of Barkers and A Area to the place of Beginning. Hereby relinquishing to him the said Richard Rowles, and his heirs and assigns forever, all the right and title in and to said land, heretofore held and possessed by the said State, And I do hereby issue this letter patent for the same. In testimony whereof I have caused the seal of the State to be affixed as well as the seal of the General land Office. Done at the City of Dublin West York In the Year of our Lord one thousand eight hundred and sixty.

J.S. Shoal Governor.
W.L. Landry Commissioner of the Gl. Land Office

NOTE ON THE CHAIN OF TITLE FROM THE PATENTEE TO THE SUBDIVISION DEVELOPER

After the patent, the title chain contains the following documents in sequence:

—warranty deed from RICHARD ROWLES et ux. to one GEORGE W. FRAZER, June 10, 1861.

—warranty deed from GEORGE W. FRAZER to Wm. R. WILSON, July 1, 1861 (this document fails to mention whether Frazer was married or to reflect joinder of his spouse).

—warranty deed from Wm. R. WILSON et ux. to HENRY HARTMANN, Nov. 9, 1861. The property was then held intact by Hartmann for many years.

These are the actual names that appear on the real conveyances (the Richard Rowles Survey is also the true name of the parcel, and it still is so called today).

Thereafter, the sequence contains literally scores of documents—a complete set of probate records in one instance, instruments creating and releasing security interests, conveyances of easements, and numerous warranty deeds. The examiner's notes that appear below are simulated from the partial record.

Ultimately, the chain wends its way to one RICHARD E. MERHITE, the developer of the Leebrook Town House Subdivision. Merhite obtained approval of a plat for development from the Planning Division of the City of London, and he conveyed to an entity called DADE CORPORATION created for the purpose of development. The following plat, reflecting the approval of the City of London, appears in the chain and is filed among the Manero County Map Records.

APPROVED PLAT OF THE LEEBROOK TOWN HOUSE SUBDIVISION

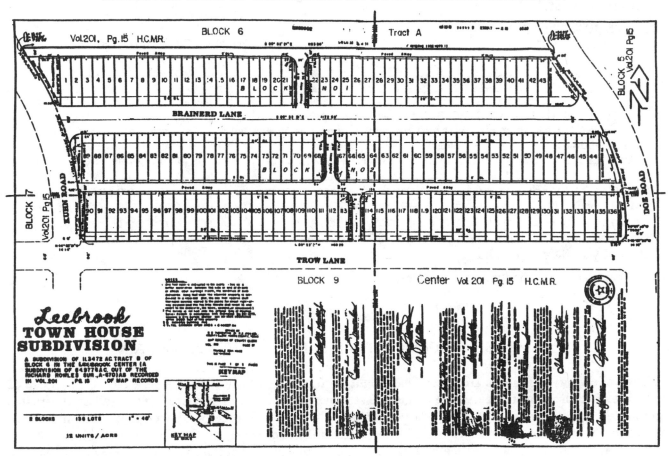

49

NOTE ON THE CHAIN OF TITLE FROM THE SUBDIVISION DEVELOPER TO PARK BANK

The chain of title includes the following documents after the plat:
—warranty deed from RICHARD MERHITE to DADE CORPORATION, a real estate investment corporation;
—declaration of covenants, conditions and restrictions upon the property executed by DADE COR- PORATION and instruments amending the declaration (excerpts from these "restrictive covenants" or "deed restrictions" appear in Chapter 7, but they also form a part of the chain of title);
—security instrument executed by DADE CORPORATION in favor of PARK BANK, to secure the loan of development funds; and
—instruments reflecting the foreclosure of that security instrument.
It appears that difficult times overcame Dade Corporation, and it was unable to repay the indebtedness to Park Bank. The following are some of the foreclosure instruments.

SECURITY INSTRUMENT (MORTGAGE) IN FAVOR OF PARK BANK

[The instrument that follows is an excerpt from the actual security instrument in the chain of title. It happens to be in the form of a deed of trust, but just as readily could have been a mortgage if located in a different State. The conveyance is to a trustee, and this excerpt reproduces that part of the document; fol- lowing paragraphs provide that the conveyance is actually for the purpose of security, provide for means of foreclosure, and set forth requirements for the borrower, Dade Corporation. Chapter 4 contains a com- plete document of this type. The documents that follow are designed to effect foreclosure in accordance with this instrument.]

THE STATE OF WEST YORK
COUNTY OF MANERO   KNOW ALL PERSONS BY THESE PRESENTS:

That the undersigned   DADE CORPORATION, a West York corporation, acting
herein by and through its duly authorized officers,   of
Manero County, West York   , hereinafter called Grantors (whether one or more), in consideration of TEN AND NO/100 DOLLARS ($10.00) cash in hand paid by   LEE JOHNSON,
hereinafter called Trustee, the receipt of which payment is hereby acknowledged and confessed, and of the debt and trust hereinafter mentioned, have Granted, Bargained, Sold and Conveyed, and by these presents to Grant, Bargain, Sell and Convey unto Trustee, and unto the successor or substitute Trustee hereinafter provided, the following described property situated in   Manero County, West York   , to-wit:

Lots Forty-Four (44) through Sixty-Seven (67), both inclusive, in Block Two (2), of LEEBROOK TOWNHOUSE SUBDIVISION, in Manero County, West York, according to the map or plat thereof re- corded in Volume 203, Page 87 of the Map Records of Manero County, West York.

[The remainder of this document is omitted.]

FORECLOSURE DOCUMENTS APPEARING IN THE TITLE CHAIN

[The following documents are those that might be found in a typical foreclosure record in a deed of trust state. Because the trustee in the original instrument is no longer easily available, a substitute trustee is appointed by the lender and is requested by the lender to act to foreclose; hence the "Appointment of Substitute Trustee and Request to Act." The trustee's functions include the posting of various notices, and the "Affidavit of Private Notice and of Posting of Public Notice of Sale" creates a document that can evidence the performance of these steps and can actually be filed of record. The trustee will have sold the property at auction at the courthouse door (the auction was probably a small group of individuals gathered about the trustee, of whom the highest bidder, as often happens, was the mortgage holder, Park Bank). Finally, the trustee gives a deed (the "Substitute Trustee's Deed," here) to the successful bidder. All of these documents are taken from the title chain in West York; in other States, slightly different documents may be required or customary. In a "straight" mortgage State, instead of these documents, there would be a petition or complaint filed in a court invoking the judicial authority to sell, a judgment of mortgage foreclosure following whatever judicial proceedings ensued, and a deed reflecting the sale of the property by a sheriff or similar officer. These documents would appear in the title chain, accomplishing the same result of transfer by foreclosure sale.]

APPOINTMENT OF SUBSTITUTE TRUSTEE AND REQUEST TO ACT

THE STATE OF WEST YORK   §
COUNTY OF MANERO   §

    WHEREAS, heretofore to-wit on the 27th day of March, A.D., _2011_, DADE CORPORATION, a West York Corporation, executed and delivered a certain Deed of Trust conveying to LEE JOHNSON, TRUSTEE, the real estate hereinafter described, to secure PARK BANK OF LONDON in payment of a debt in said Deed of Trust described, said Deed of Trust being recorded in volume 200, page 146, of the Official Deed Records of Manero County, West York, and
    WHEREAS, default has occurred in the payment of said indebtedness, and by reason of such default the indebtedness in said Deed of Trust described is now wholly due; and
    WHEREAS, LEE JOHNSON, the Trustee in said Deed of Trust named, is absent and/or has resigned and/or refused to act as said Trustee, and has so certified to PARK BANK OF LONDON, the legal owner and holder of the indebtedness secured in said Deed of Trust;
    NOW, THEREFORE, KNOW ALL PERSONS BY THESE PRESENTS: That in consideration of the premises, the legal owner and holder of the above described indebtedness, does hereby NAME, CONSTITUTE AND APPOINT W. D. STONES, of Manero County, West York, as Substitute Trustee under said Deed of Trust, under the provisions of said Deed of Trust and as provided therein, and further, does hereby request the said W. D. STONES, Substitute Trustee, to sell such property to satisfy said indebtedness; said property being described as follows, to-wit:
        Lots Forty-four (44) through Sixty-seven (67), both inclusive, in Block Two (2) of LEEBROOK TOWNHOUSE SUBDIVISION, an addition in Manero County, West York, according to the map or plat thereof, recorded in Volume 203, Page 87, of the Map Records of Manero County, West York.
EXECUTED this the 6th day of February, A.D., _2013_.

[Attestation and acknowledgement omitted.]   PARK BANK OF LONDON

                                     By: *Michael E. Way*
                                 MICHAEL E. WAY, VICE-PRESIDENT

AFFIDAVIT OF PRIVATE NOTICE AND OF POSTING OF PUBLIC NOTICE OF SALE

THE STATE OF WEST YORK   §
COUNTY OF MANERO   §

    BEFORE ME, the undersigned authority, on this day personally appeared W. D. STONES, to me well known to be a credible person and qualified in all respects to make this Affidavit, who being first by me duly sworn, upon oath says:

On the dates listed below Notice of Substitute Trustee's Sale on the property described on the attached Exhibit "A", being the same property described in instrument filed in volume 200, page 146, of the Deed Records of Manero County, West York, was posted in accordance with the requirements of law and in accordance with the said instrument, at the Courthouse Door of Manero County, at 6:00 o'clock P.M., February 6, 2013.

On February 6, 2013, Notice of the acceleration and foreclosure was mailed by certified mail to Dade Corporation and Richard B. Merhite, and on February 11, 2013, they received said Notice according to the return receipt card numbers 761338 and 761340.

W D Stones
W. D. STONES
___

SUBSCRIBED AND SWORN TO BEFORE ME, by the said W.D. STONES, this the _6th_ day of February, A.D.,   , to certify which witness my Hand and Seal of Office.

[Acknowledgement omitted.]

Bullard P Ferrington
Notary Public in and for
Manero County, West York

SUBSTITUTE TRUSTEE'S DEED

| THE STATE OF WEST YORK | § | KNOW ALL PERSONS BY THESE PRESENTS: |
| COUNTY OF MANERO | § | |

WHEREAS, on the 27th day of March, 2011, DADE CORPORATION, a West York Corporation, did execute and deliver to PARK BANK OF LONDON, of the County of Manero and the State of West York, one certain promissory note in the original principal amount of SEVEN HUNDRED SEVENTY-THOUSAND AND NO/100 DOLLARS ($770,000.00), said note bearing interest at the rate of sixteen percent (16%) per annum, reference to which note is here made for all purposes; and * * *

[The instrument here recites the events underlying the foreclosure, including execution of the deed of trust, borrower's default in payment, appointment of the substitute trustee, notice, acceleration, etc.]

WHEREAS, there is now due on said note the amount of SEVEN HUNDRED EIGHT THOUSAND SEVEN HUNDRED NINE AND 94/100 DOLLARS ($708,709.94), plus accrued interest and attorney's fees as therein provided; and,

WHEREAS, the said W. D. STONES, SUBSTITUTE TRUSTEE as aforesaid, in compliance with the request of the holder of said note, and in accordance with the law, did give legal notice of Trustee's sale by posting notice thereof for the time and in the manner provided in said Deed of Trust, in accordance with law, and did offer said property for sale at public auction at the door of the courthouse of Manero County, West York, in the City of London, West York, on the 5th day of April, 2013, the same being the first Tuesday of said month, between the hours of 10:00 A.M. and 4:00 P.M., to the highest bidder, for cash, and said property was at such sale, knocked off to PARK BANK OF LONDON for the sum of FIVE HUNDRED SIXTY-SIX THOUSAND NINE HUNDRED SIXTY-SEVEN AND 95/100 DOLLARS ($566,967.95), the said PARK BANK OF LONDON being the highest and best bidder therefor;

NOW, THEREFORE, KNOW ALL PERSONS BY THESE PRESENTS:

That I, W. D. STONES, SUBSTITUTE TRUSTEE, as aforesaid, by virtue
of the power and authority vested in me as such Substitute Trustee,
for and in consideration of the premises and the sum of FIVE HUNDRED
SIXTY-SIX THOUSAND NINE HUNDRED SIXTY-SEVEN AND 95/100 DOLLARS
($566,967.95), cash, to me in hand paid by PARK BANK OF LONDON, the
receipt of which is hereby fully acknowledged and confessed, do by
these presents, GRANT, SELL AND CONVEY to the said PARK BANK OF
LONDON the following described property, to-wit:
  Lots Forty-four (44) through Sixty-seven (67), both inclusive,
  in Block Two (2) of LEEBROOK TOWNHOUSE SUBDIVISION, * * *
TO HAVE AND TO HOLD the above described property, together with
all and singular the rights and appurtenances thereto and anywise
belonging, unto PARK BANK OF LONDON, its successors and assigns, forever, in fee simple, and I, the said W. D. STONES, SUBSTITUTE
TRUSTEE, do hereby bind the said DADE CORPORATION, its successors
and assigns, to WARRANT AND FOREVER DEFEND, the right and title to
said property to the said PARK BANK OF LONDON, its successors and
assigns forever, against every person whomsoever lawfully claiming
or to claim the same, or any part thereof.
  EXECUTED this the 5th day of April, 2013.

                                    W D Stones
[Acknowledgement omitted.]   _____
                                    W.D. STONES, SUBSTITUTE TRUSTEE

B. TITLE EXAMINATION AND OPINION

EXAMINER'S NOTES (EXCERPTS)

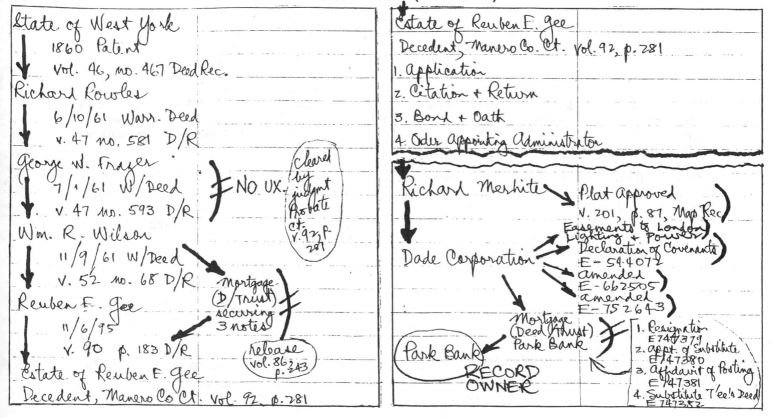

CERTIFICATION OF ABSENCE OF TAX LIENS

TAX CERTIFICATE

STATE OF WEST YORK   §   Prepared for: *McIntosh & Walker*

COUNTY OF MANERO   §   Current year tax: _____

    I, Raymond B. Bradley, Tax Assessor-Collector for Manero County, West York, hereby certify that I (or my Deputy), have made a careful check of the Tax Records of Manero County, West York up to and including the year 19___ and did not find a record of any taxes due against the following Property except for the years:

    ALL PAID

Amount current $ *NONE*   Delinquent $ *NONE*   Total $ *NONE*

Lot or Abstract	Block or Acres	Addition or Survey
65	2	*Leebrook Town House Subdivision*

Rendered in the name of *Park Bank of London* for the year *2013*.

    This certificate is issued in compliance with and subject to the provisions of article 7258B, Civil Statutes, Chapter 339, Acts of the 61st. Legislature 1969, and the fee of $2.00 is charged for issuing same, as provided in said law.

    Our delinquent rolls are public records, and open to any taxpayer or abstract & title company who wishes to check them.

    Dated this ___*18*___ day of ___*April*___, *2014*.

by: *E. Brenda Landon* , Deputy   Raymond B. Bradley
                                  Tax Assessor-Collector, Manero County

---

CERTIFICATION OF ABSENCE OF JUDGMENT LIENS

JUDGMENT LIEN CERTIFICATE

    We hereby certify that we have examined the indices to the records for twenty (20) years last past to date*, unless otherwise noted herein, and find no Judgment, Attachment, Decree, Order on Mandate, Recognizance, Receivership action, or other lien: nor any Proceedings in Bankruptcy remain open or unsatisfied of record in lien docket in the Superior Court of the State of West York and the United States District Court for the District of West York except as below set forth against: Park Bank of London: NONE

*(Receivership actions are certified up to FOUR days prior to the date herein.)

Fee $ 18.20   Signed at 8:55 A.M. on April 5, *2014*

Copy $

To: Robert L. Livingston   SUPERIOR TITLE SEARCH COMPANY
      McIntosh & Walker   By *Candace Epstein*
      First City National Bank Bldg.   PRESIDENT
      London, W.Y.   77002

TITLE OPINION

    [Practice with respect to title examination varies greatly from jurisdiction to jurisdiction. In some jurisdictions, no attorney would examine the title; instead, non-attorney examiners, skilled in the methods of title evaluation, would be employed by title insurer for the task. If there were a title opinion by an attorney, it might be based upon an abstract of title prepared by a non-lawyer abstractor as is the one illustrated below. An abstractor examines the official records and furnishes the lawyer with copies or summaries of the instruments in the chain of title. In some States, lawyers perform the abstracting role.]

McINTOSH & WALKER
Attorneys at Law
First City National Bank Bldg.
London, West York 77002
April 22, 2014

RE: TITLE OPINION, Lot 65, Block 2, Leebrook Town House Subdivision
Mr. Edgar E. Pynes and Mr. Andrew B. Pynes
43 Sandra Circle #3A
London, West York 77040

Dear Sirs:

The writer has examined, at your request, title to the above described real property, as reflected by the following abstracts of title:
1) Manero County Abstract Company, Abstract No. 7290, containing 121 pages and Certificate, commencing with Grant from the State of West York dated post July 7, 1860 and closing September 6, 1980 at 8:00 P.M.
2) Manero County Abstract Company, Supplemental Abstract No. 15211, containing 27 pages and Certificate, commencing September 6, 1980 and closing April 20, 2014 at 8:00 A.M.

BASED UPON EXAMINATION OF THE FOREGOING, the writer finds marketable title to such property in Park Bank of London, a West York corporation, subject to the following:
    1. Declaration of Covenants, Conditions and Restrictions set forth in instrument filed of record under Manero County Clerk's file no. E-544072, as amended by instruments filed of record under file nos. E-662505 and E-752643, including all assessments, easements, incumbrances, and interests thereby created or recognized.

[Here the opinion sets out each of the encumbrances found. The list is identical to items 5 through 7 of the exceptions to the Title Commitment, below, and reflects the items marked in the examiner's notes, above.]

SUGGESTION

The writer suggests that you familiarize yourself with the same and the extent to which they apply to your use of such property, and if the location of or type of improvements violate the same.
    4. Driveway Easement: Appurtenant to Lot 64, Block 2, Leebrook Town Homes Subdivision. The survey, on its face, shows that the property contains a common driveway with the named Lot 64. From the record, an examiner can infer the possibility of creation in the owner of the abutting property of an easement or other interest in the use of the Driveway but cannot ascertain the existence or nature of such interest.

REQUIREMENT

It will be the writer's requirement that any such easement or other interest be conveyed to the Record Owner by an instrument filed of Record.***

EXCEPTIONS AND LIMITATIONS

The writer has not examined the property on the grounds to ascertain whether the legal description as given is correct, or whether the same contains the represented quantity of land, whether boundary encroachments exist, or whether improvements violate the subdivision set-back and building lines. The currently available survey is not adequate for those purposes; a survey certified as having been made on the ground, with all corners monumented, is necessary to determine the foregoing. The writer has further not examined the property with respect to rights of parties in possession, liens for labor and materials, or easements, equitable servitudes, or similar interests not of record.

Very truly yours,
McINTOSH & WALKER
by: *Robert L. Livingston*
    Robert L. Livingston

C. NOTES AND QUESTIONS ON TITLE EXAMINATION

1. **TITLE SEARCH BACK TO THE SOVEREIGN.** Why is it necessary for the examiner, in this jurisdiction, to trace title back to the sovereign? (Hint: if the patentee had made another recorded grant, prior to the first grantee in this chain, and if the current record owner were unable to demonstrate a long enough period of adverse possession to establish title, what would be the state of the title?)

2. **ADVERSE POSSESSION AS BOTH A SWORD AND A SHIELD IN TITLE WORK.** Limitation title (or title by adverse possession) is both a blessing and a nuisance to the title examiner. In very old grants, loose ends in the form of marital property rights and the like are sometimes cured by adverse possession. But recent adverse possession by a person outside the title chain would present the possibility that the current record owner does not have title. Notice that the opinion expressly excludes this consideration (as does the title insurance policy below).

3. **THE PUTATIVE "DRIVEWAY EASEMENT."** Can you see why the common driveway creates a problem? Might it constitute a way of necessity? A prescriptive easement? Or nothing at all? (Hint: the strong likelihood is that there is no such easement, but would an insurer so insure, and should an attorney seeing the survey omit it?)

4. **THE EXAMINER'S METHODOLOGY.** The examiner has used documents provided by an abstract company and certified by it as containing all documents of record affecting the property. It is customary for these documents to be contained in a "base" volume, covering the chain from the sovereign to the person platting the subdivision (this volume then can be used for each lot in the subdivision), and a "supplemental" volume covering the particular lot. The examiner indicates each transfer of any interest by an arrow. He draws a bold half-circle when he finds a potential defect. Several of these half-circles are struck through or crossed out, indicating that subsequent instruments in the chain have cleared them (as in the case of a release of a mortgage). When the chain reaches the current record owner, the half-circles that have not been crossed out are the encumbrances that remain upon the property.

5. **MARKETABLE TITLE LEGISLATION.** In a State with marketable title legislation, this process would be considerably simplified. Marketable title laws generally provide that (with certain exceptions) a person who can show a chain of record title for a period of time (which may be 30, 40, or 50 years) has marketable title. It is not ordinarily necessary to trace to the sovereign in a State with a marketable title statute. Rather, the examiner may be able to trace backward (with limited forward steps) for only the period required by the statute.

6. **MARKETABLE TITLE, RECORD TITLE, AND INDEFEASIBLE TITLE.** What if there are two conflicting chains of title in a State with marketable title legislation (as might happen if a grantor in the chain made two inconsistent grants or if a chain was created by adverse possession)? In that event, the holder of "marketable title" may (or may not) prevail. Furthermore, certain interests, including mineral

rights, are not affected by marketable title legislation. Thus if the true state of the title is crucially important and cannot be adequately insured (if the record owner plans to drill an oil well, for example), the marketable title statute may not provide enough protection, and a complete examination back to the sovereign may be undertaken. The ordinary residential transaction does not present such a case.

7. THE RECORDING SYSTEM AND TITLE EXAMINATION. In a State without marketable title legislation, title insurers or abstract companies often maintain extensive private collections of documents duplicating public records—but arranged by tract. The public record system with its grantor-grantee index may be too cumbersome to use in such a State. But in States with marketable title legislation, public records accessed through the grantor-grantee and reverse indexes may be sufficient. In a few States, the official records are maintained and indexed by tract.

8. TAXES AND JUDGMENTS. Why is it important that tax and judgment records be searched? (Can you see why the title-search-and-insurance process can be a valuable aid to debt collectors?) Incidentally, certificates were obtained from the city of London, the school district, and all other taxing authorities, not just from the county.

9. JURISDICTIONAL VARIATIONS AND THE ROLE OF ATTORNEYS. Title records, governing law, and customary practices vary sharply from State to State. In States with marketable title legislation, examination by an attorney is more common. The attorney may be acting for the buyer (in which event the custom may be for the lender and insurer to rely upon his title opinion, effectively making the buyer's attorney liable to them for defects that he negligently fails to discover). Or the attorney may act directly on behalf of the lender or insurer, who may have approved lists of attorneys. Finally, in many jurisdictions it is customary for title insurance to be based upon the title company's in-house examination, with no attorney involved at all.

D. THE TITLE INSURANCE COMMITMENT, TITLE "CURING," AND THE TITLE POLICY

COMMITMENT FOR TITLE INSURANCE

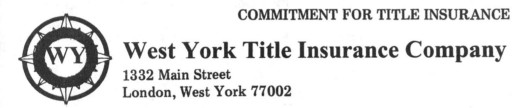

West York Title Insurance Company

1332 Main Street
London, West York 77002

AGREEMENT TO ISSUE POLICY

We agree to issue a policy to you according to the terms of this Commitment. When we show the policy amount and your name as the proposed insured in Schedule A, this Commitment becomes effective as of the Commitment Date shown in Schedule A.

If the Requirements shown in this Commitment have not been met within nine (9) months after the Commitment Date, our obligation under this Commitment will end. Also, our obligation under this Commitment will end when the Policy is issued and then our obligation to you will be under the Policy.

Our obligation under this Commitment is limited by the following:

The provisions in Schedule A.
The Requirements in Schedule B-I.
The Exceptions in Schedule B-II.
The Conditions on reverse side of cover.

This Commitment is not valid without SCHEDULE A and Sections I and II of Schedule B.

IN WITNESS WHEREOF WEST YORK TITLE INSURANCE COMPANY has caused this Commitment to be signed and sealed as of the effective date shown in Schedule a; the Commitment to become valid when countersigned by an authorized signatory.

[CONDITIONS: The first section of the Commitment, called "conditions," contains definitions, provisos, and limitations. This section empowers the insurer to add defects that arise after the commitment but before issuance of the policy, or defects known to the insured but not disclosed. It purports to limit obligations to issuance of the policy and to limit liability, if any, for errors in the commitment to actual loss within policy limits.

[Schedule A indicates that an owner's policy is to be issued for $834,200 to the Pyneses, and a mortgagee's policy for $834,200 is to be issued to Huntington Savings. It reflects that "fee simple interest in the land described in this Commitment is owned . . . by Park Bank of London."]

schedule b –section I – requirements

The following requirements must be met:

(a)   Pay the agreed amounts for the interest in the land and/or the mortgage to be insured.

(b)   Pay us the premiums, fees and charges for the policy.

(c)   You must tell us in writing the name of anyone not referred to in this Commitment who will get an interest in the land or who will make a loan on the land. We may then make additional requirements or exceptions.

(d)   Documents satisfactory to us creating the interest in the land and/or the mortgage to be insured must be signed, delivered and recorded:

(1)   Deed from Park Bank of London to Edgar E. Pynes and Andrew B. Pynes.

(2)   Deed of Trust or Mortgage from Edgar E. Pynes and Andrew B. Pynes in favor of Huntington Savings Association.

(3)   Documents satisfactory to us extinguishing, releasing or conveying to Park Bank of London any easement, equitable servitude or other interest appurtenant to Lot 64, Block 2, of the same subdivision by reason of common drive.

In addition to the above Requirements, the following items will appear as exceptions to coverage in any policy we issue unless they are taken care of to our satisfaction:

1.   Proof as to past and present marital status of present owner and buyer.

2.   Taxes and municipal claims.   deleted. See Attached Certificates.

3.   Possible additional assessment for real property taxes.

4.   Possible liability for municipal improvements such as curbing, paving, sidewalks, sewers, etc., constructed or being constructed, but not assessed. deleted. See Attached Certificates.

5.   State   Superior Court and United States District Court judgments and bankruptcies.
           See Attached Search Certificate.

None [X]   Shown hereon or attached [ ]   Supplemental Report will follow [ ]

Any policy we issue will have the following exceptions unless they are taken care of to our satisfaction.

1. Rights or claims of parties in possession of the land not shown by the public record.
2. Easements, or claims of easements, not shown by the public record.
3. Any facts about the land which a correct survey would disclose, and which are not shown by the public record.
4. Any liens on your title, arising now or later, for labor and material, not shown by the public record.

5. Declaration of Covenants, Conditions, and Restrictions set forth in instrument filed of record under Manero County Clerk's file no. E-544072, as amended by instruments filed of record under file nos. E-662505 and E-752643, including all assessments, easements, incumbrances and interests thereby created or recognized.

6. All easements, rights-of-way, and building lines as shown on the plat of Leebrook Town House Subdivision, as recorded in volume 203, page 87, of the Map Records of Manero County.

7. Those certain easements granted to London Power & Light Co., by instruments filed of record under Manero County Clerk's file nos. E-438703, E-509174, and E-509175.

[Schedule C contains the legal description of the land insured. Certain other parts of the commitment are omitted.]

C.T. 96 ALTA COMMITMENT
NJRB 3-02

BOUNDARY AGREEMENT CURING PUTATIVE "DRIVEWAY EASEMENT"

DRIVEWAY AGREEMENT

This agreement, entered into this 29th day of May, 1984, by and between Park Bank of London, a banking corporation chartered under the laws of the State of West York (hereinafter referred to as BANK), and Matthew C. Rabin and Mary Ann Rabin, his wife, residing at 7949 Brainerd Lane, London, Manero County, West York (hereinafter referred to as RABIN), WITNESSETH THAT:

WHEREAS, BANK and RABIN are the owners of adjoining premises located in London, Manero County, West York, the lands of BANK being more specifically described as Lot 65, Block 2, Leebrook Town House Subdivision, an addition to the City of London, West York, and the lands of RABIN being more specifically described as Lot 64, Block 2, of the same Leebrook Town House Subdivision, both as shown on the Map or Plat thereof recorded in volume 203, page 87 of the Map Records of Manero County, West York; and

WHEREAS, the driveways of lands of BANK and lands of RABIN abut each other and, by virtue thereof, constitute a double driveway not separated by a fence or any other evidence of division; and

WHEREAS, it is the desire of the parties to document of record in the Office of the County Clerk of Manero County, West York, that neither party has any interest by way of common driveway in lands of the other;

NOW, THEREFORE, for and in consideration of the sum of One ($1.00) Dollar each to the other in hand paid, the receipt of which is hereby acknowledged, the parties hereto do agree as follows:

That the division line between the parties as described on the Map or Plat recorded in the Office of the County Clerk of Manero County, West York as aforementioned, delineates in all respects the division line between the parties hereto and neither asserts on the lands of the other a right of ingress and egress, or for parking, or any other interest, and that each party to this agreement exclusively utilizes his own lands for purposes of ingress and egress and parking.

IN WITNESS WHEREOF, the parties have set their hands and seals the day and year first above written.

[Signatures and acknowledgements are omitted.]

EXCERPTS FROM TITLE INSURANCE POLICY

West York Title Insurance Company
1332 Main Street
London, West York 77002 　　　* * *

COVERED RISKS

SUBJECT TO THE EXCLUSIONS FROM COVERAGE, THE EXCEPTIONS FROM COVERAGE CONTAINED IN SCHEDULE B AND THE CONDITIONS, **THE WEST YORK** LAND TITLE INSURANCE COMPANY, a Nebraska corporation (the "Company") insures, as of Date of Policy and, to the extent stated in Covered Risks 9 and 10, after Date of Policy, against loss or damage, not exceeding the Amount of Insurance, sustained or incurred by the Insured by reason of:

1. Title being vested other than as stated in Schedule A.
2. Any defect in or lien or encumbrance on the Title. This Covered Risk includes but is not limited to insurance against loss from:
   (a) A defect in the Title caused by:
      (i) forgery, fraud, undue influence, duress, incompetency, incapacity, or impersonation;
      (ii) failure of any person or Entity to have authorized a transfer or conveyance;
      (iii) a document affecting Title not properly created, executed, witnessed, sealed, acknowledged, notarized or delivered;
      (iv) failure to perform those acts necessary to create a document by electronic means authorized by law;
      (v) a document executed under a falsified, expired or otherwise invalid power of attorney;
      (vi) a document not properly filed, recorded or indexed in the Public Records including failure to perform those acts by electronic means authorized by law; or
      (vii) a defective judicial or administrative proceeding.
   (b) The lien of real estate taxes or assessments imposed on the Title by a governmental authority due or payable, but unpaid.
   (c) Any encroachment, encumbrance, violation, variation, or adverse circumstance affecting the Title that would be disclosed by an accurate and complete land survey of the Land. The term "encroachment" includes encroachments of existing improvements located on the Land onto adjoining land, and encroachments onto the Land of existing improvements located on adjoining land.
   (d) Any statutory or constitutional mechanic's, contractor's, or materialman's lien for labor or materials having its inception on or before Date of Policy.
3. Lack of good and indefeasible Title.
4. No right of access to and from the Land. * * *

COMPANY'S DUTY TO DEFEND AGAINST COURT CASES

We will defend your title in any court case that is based on a matter insured against by this Policy. We will pay the costs, attorneys' fees, and expenses we incur in that defense.

We can end this duty to defend your title by exercising any of our options listed in Item 4 of the Conditions.

* * *

SCHEDULE A

Name and address of title insurance company: **West York Title Insurance Company, Box 45000, Omaha Nebraska 85138** * * *

Amount of insurance: **$ 834,200.00**

Premium: **$ 4,764.00**

Date of policy: **June 30, 2014** * * *

The estate or interest in the land that is insured by this policy is: **fee simple absolute**

Title is vested in: **Edgar E. Pynes and Adnrew B. Pynes**

The land is described as follows: **Lot 65, Block 2, of Leebrook Town House Subdivision, a subdivision in Manero County, West York.**

SCHEDULE B: EXCEPTIONS

In addition to the Exclusions, you are not insured against loss, costs, attorneys' fees, and expenses resulting from:

[The exceptions that were to be found in Schedule B II of the Commitment are set out at this point, in typewritten form.]

EXCLUSIONS

[A standard list of exclusions is attached, covering exercises of the governmental police power; condemnation; risks agreed to, known to, or resulting in no loss to, the policyholder; failure to pay value for the title; and lack of rights in land outside the description or in streets, alleys or waterways.]

CONDITIONS
* * *

4. OUR CHOICES WHEN YOU NOTIFY US OF A CLAIM

After we receive your claim notice or in any other way learn of a matter for which we are liable, we can do one or more of the following:

a. Pay the claim against your title.

b. Negotiate a settlement.

c. Prosecute or defend a court case related to the claim.

d. Pay you the amount required by this Policy.

e. Take other action which will protect you.

f. Cancel this Policy by paying the Policy Amount, then in force, and only those costs, attorneys' fees and expenses incurred up to that time which we are obligated to pay.

* * *

6. LIMITATION OF THE COMPANY'S LIABILITY

a. We will pay up to your actual loss or the Policy Amount in force when the claim is made—whichever is less.

b. If we remove the claim against your title within a reasonable time after receiving notice of it, we will
have no further liability for it.

If you cannot use any of your land because of a claim against your title, and you rent reasonable substitute land or facilities, we will repay you for your actual rent until:

- the cause of the claim is removed

or

- we settle your claim.

c. The Policy Amount will be reduced by all payments made under this Policy—except for costs, attorneys' fees and expenses.

d. The Policy Amount will be reduced by any amount we pay to our insured holder of any mortgage
shown in this Policy or a later mortgage given by you.

e. If you do anything to affect any right of recovery you may have, we can subtract from our liability the
amount by which you reduced the value of that right.

* * *

8. OUR LIABILITY IS LIMITED TO THIS POLICY

This Policy, plus any endorsements, is the entire contract between you and the Company. Any title
claim you make against us must be made under this Policy and is subject to its terms.

E. NOTES AND QUESTIONS ON TITLE CURING AND TITLE INSURANCE

1. THE FUNCTION OF TITLE INSURANCE. People buy most kinds of insurance for indemnity
against loss. But potential indemnity is not the only incentive for purchasing title insurance. If a title
company is willing to issue a policy insuring a certain interest in land, that is sufficient indication for most
residential purchasers (and for many commercial ones as well) that the purchase can be made with confidence in the status of the title.

2. WHAT THE POLICY INSURES. What are the insurer's obligations under the Commitment and
under the Policy? It is interesting to note that the insurer's liability is both broader and narrower than
that of a title examiner such as an attorney. What if the title chain contains a forgery, or a wild deed
results in loss to the grantee? A title insurance company would be liable for the loss, but an attorney who
examined the title would not be liable (unless he was negligent or warranted title). But what if the value
of the property appreciates enormously before the absence of title is discovered (e.g., buyer builds a
$100,000 structure on a $10,000 parcel of land)? The insurer's liability is confined by the policy limits,
but the liability of a negligent examiner is not.

3. THE COMMITMENT (OR POLICY) AS A CONTRACT AND AS A REPRESENTATION. The
title insurer is anxious to limit its liability, if it can, to the contract itself. But given the reliance of most
buyers on insurance as the basis for confidence in the title, would it surprise you if a buyer were to try to
hold the insurer liable under warranty, negligence or other theories if his loss exceeded the policy limits?
Some States have recognized such liability, while others have not.

4. TITLE CURING: THE BOUNDARY AGREEMENT CLEARING THE PUTATIVE "DRIVEWAY
EASEMENT." The "Driveway Agreement" is an interesting example of the interplay between theoretical
concepts and pragmatism. If an interest or encumbrance actually appears to exist, the theoretically most
satisfying way to deal with it is to release or convey it, and quitclaim deeds or other conveyances are in
fact often used in title curing. But what would have been the reaction of the neighbor in Lot 64, if he had
been approached by Park Bank with the request that he make a conveyance to the Bank? Another way to

deal with the problem is to file an instrument of record, extinguishing the encumbrance by agreeing that it does not exist. From the neighbor's perspective, this instrument is understandable, it is mutual, and he is more likely to sign it.

5. **TITLE CURING BY AFFIDAVIT.** What if there were judgments of record in names similar to that of the grantor (a common situation)? What about marital property, potential construction liens, etc.? The common practice is for the grantor to execute an "Affidavit of Title" in a form such as the following:

AFFIDAVIT OF TITLE

* * *

3. OWNERSHIP AND POSSESSION. We are the only owners of the described property. We now sell this property to the Buyers. We are in sole possession of this property. There are no tenants or other occupants of this property. We have owned this property since [Date]. Since then no one has questioned our ownership or right to possession. * * *

[Paragraphs denying recent construction to negate the possibility of liens for labor and materials), and denying other encumbrances, are omitted.]

6. MARITAL HISTORY. (check where appropriate)

☐ We are not married.

☐ We are married to each other. We were married on [Date]. The birth name of [Wife] was [Name].

☐ This property has never been occupied as the principal matrimonial residence of any of us. (If it has, each spouse must sign the deed and affidavit.)

☐ Our complete marital history is listed below under paragraph number 7.* * *

7. EXCEPTIONS AND ADDITIONS. The following is a complete list of exceptions and additions to the above statements. This includes all liens or mortgages which are not being paid off as a result of this sale.

> Our attention has been directed to the Judgment Search of West York Title Search Company, a copy of which is attached hereto. The judgments therein contained are not against us but against others of similar name.

[Execution and certain other provisions omitted.]

6. **OBTAINING A MODIFIED OR EXTENDED TITLE INSURANCE POLICY.** Suppose that the buyer is troubled by a particular exception contained in the Title Commitment. As an example, imagine that he wants to remove the exception for "facts about the land which a correct survey would disclose." (He might be concerned about that common exception if, for example, the property was particularly valuable or if he had reason to suspect that the survey would disclose errors or encroachments, etc.) Consider the following:

```
FROM: McINTOSH & WALKER        TO: PAUL SMITH SURVEY ASSOCIATES
June 8, 2014                       101 Dublin Ave., London WY 77056

Gentlemen:
    Receipt is acknowledged of your survey Dated May 31,
on premises at 7949 Brainerd Lane, London, W.Y. and also your
duplicate bill. The requisition letter requested a staked sur-
vey. We can use the location survey to prepare for closing, but
mark your records to go back to install the stakes (and resub-
mit your invoice taking into account the setting of such stakes)
so that we can remove the survey exception from the Title Policy.
McINTOSH & WALKER
by: Robert I. Livingston
```

Upon receipt of a properly monumented survey, and upon payment of an appropriate premium, the title insurer would be in a position to delete the survey exception by an endorsement such as the one that follows.

SURVEY ENDORSEMENT (Plain Language)

Exception number 1 in Schedule B of this policy is deleted and the following is substituted:

1. Based upon a survey made by **Paul Smith Survey Associates,**

dated **June 12, 2014,** the Company hereby insures you against loss or damage which you suffer by reason of any encroachments, overlaps, boundary line disputes or easements, except as follows:

None.

This endorsement is a part of your policy or commitment. Nothing else in your policy or commitment changes.

CHAPTER SIX:

THE CLOSING

In most transactions involving items of significant value or complexity, there are many legal instruments that must be executed at or about the same time, and the instruments are usually drafted in advance and executed at a predetermined time and place. This ceremony, set in motion in this case by the contract of purchase and sale, is called a "closing."

The closing in this case (as in most instances involving sale of real estate in West York) took place in the offices of the title insurance company. In other States, the more common practice is for it to be held at a lawyer's office.

In many instances, both seller and buyer meet at the closing to execute the documents together (as well as work out unresolved problems). In this case, however, the parties closed separately, at different times (the bank officer who executed the documents apparently did so at the offices of the bank). The purchaser was given a specific time—2:30 p.m. on Thursday, June 30, 2014—to appear for the closing, which was held in the office of one of the title company's agents (called, appropriately enough, a "closer"). The closing required certain explanations, payments and the writing and re-writing of an escrow agreement. It took about an hour and a half to accomplish these steps and for the purchaser to read and execute the note, deed of trust and other instruments.

A. LENDER'S CLOSING INSTRUCTIONS

LETTER FROM LENDER TO CLOSER

[The lender typically insists on certain procedures at closing as a condition of its funding of the loan. The instructions may be in a printed, fill-in-the blank form; here they take the form of a letter from lender's counsel. The loan will be funded and payments based upon it made after closing in conformity with the instructions.]

CORTELLI & BARNES
Attorneys and Counselors

Ms. Rhonda Gaines, West York Title Company
2300 Northwest Freeway
London, West York 77627

June 21, 2014

 Re: Huntington Savings Association ("Lender") $ 600,000 Loan to
  Edgar E. Pynes, a baron sole and Andrew B. Pynes ("Borrowers");
  Your GF No. 71283

Dear Ms. Gaines:

 Our client, Lender, is prepared to make a purchase money loan in the exact amount of Six Hundred Thousand Dollars and no/100 Dollars ($ 600,000) to Borrowers ("Loan"). The loan will be evidenced by a

Promissory Note which will be secured in part by a first lien Deed of Trust on the property described in your Commitment for Title Insurance ("Commitment") issued under the above referenced GF number ("Property").

You will act as closing, insuring and escrow officer in accordance with the instructions contained in this letter. Enclosed please find the original and one (1) copy of the following instruments for your use in this transaction:

1. General Warranty Deed to be executed by Seller;
2. Tax Notice to be executed by Borrowers;
3. UCC-1 Financing Statement to be executed by Borrowers;
4. Promissory Note to be executed by Borrowers;
5. Deed of Trust (with Adjustable Rate Rider and PUD Rider) securing the Promissory Note to be executed by Borrowers;
6. Regulation Z (Truth-in-Lending) Disclosure Form to be executed by Borrowers;
7. HUD-1 Form and Addendum to be executed by Borrowers;

[The list is lengthy, and other items are omitted here.]

You are to comply with the following instructions in closing this Loan.

1. Please collect at closing full payment for the following items:
   a. Our fee for legal services which is evidenced by the enclosed statements;
   b. Your premium for a Mortgagee Policy of Title Insurance in the amount of the Loan;
   c. Lender's origination fee in the amount of One Thousand Two Hundred Fifty Dollars ($ 1,250) from Buyer);
   d. Lender's PMI fee in the amount of Four Hundred Three and 50/100 Dollars ($ 403.50);

   [Other items for collection are omitted here.]

2. Please have the enclosed instruments executed in accordance with the following instructions:
   a. Have all instruments executed by the appropriate parties;
   b. Have all pages of the instruments initialed by the party executing that instrument;

[The closer is to assure that all acknowledgements are proper, all instruments are dated with the same date, etc.]

No corrections or additions shall be made to any instrument without my express consent.

3. After execution and your review, please comply with the following instructions:
   a. Record the following instruments with the appropriate recording agents:

   [The deed and mortgage instruments are here described.]

   b. Issue your Mortgagee Policy of Title Insurance ("Mortgagee Policy") insuring Lender a valid first lien in the amount of the Loan, and subject only to those title matters set forth in the Commitment under Schedule B II, Paragraphs 1, 2, 4, and 5 through 7. Except only to taxes for the year 1984 and subsequent years not yet due and payable. Delete the standard printed exception for discrepancies in boundary lines (except for area shortages) at Borrowers' expense.
   c. Deliver the following documents and three (3) certified

copies to Ms. Bonnie Grimes of Lender at 2530 Winston, London, West York 77063, with copies to me:
1. Mortgagee Policy;
2. Certified copy of Borrowers' Closing Statement;
[Other listed documents are omitted here.]
  d. Deliver an executed copy of these closing instructions directly to me.
  e. After the recorded instruments have been returned by the recording agents, forward the original Deed of Trust to Ms. Bonnie Grimes, with a copy to me. Forward certified copies of Releases of Liens, if any, and the General Warranty Deed to Ms. Bonnie Grimes with copies to me.
  f. Lender will advance to you the Loan proceeds. You are authorized to disburse the proceeds when you are in a position to insure Lender a valid first lien against the Property.

We and our client, Lender, understand, and by execution of this letter you warrant to us, that all title matters and information have been checked by you to the date of closing and that your recording of the documents evidencing this transaction will signify to us that the terms and conditions contained in the Mortgagee Policy will be written by you in accordance with the instructions contained in this letter with no additional exceptions or modifications of any nature except for the liens arising in connection with this Loan.

In the event you have any questions about any matter contained in this letter, please do not hesitate to contact me.

Very truly yours,
CORTELLI & BARNES
Robert E. Bowles
Robert E. Bowles

Enclosures

ACCEPTED, ACKNOWLEDGED AND AGREED
to this the __30th__ day of __June, 2014__
West York Title Insurance Company
By: __Rhonda Gaines__
Name: __RHONDA GAINES__
Title: __CLOSER__

B. RESOLVING LOOSE ENDS AT THE CLOSING: NEGOTIATION OF A SPECIAL ESCROW ACCOUNT

DISCUSSIONS BETWEEN BUYER AND HIS BROKER

Before the closing, the purchaser and his broker met, and a conversation similar to the following occurred:

Purchaser: What problems could there be if the closer doesn't know about the escrow fund?

Broker: Paperwork's all supposed to be done. I don't think we'll have any problems with the other side. They want the deal.

This conversation concerned an escrow account agreed to between the buyer and the seller to secure the seller's performance of certain repair and cleanup work, consisting primarily of matters raised in the engineering inspection report (see chapter 3). The broker had suggested this solution as an alternative to delaying the transaction. It had been arranged in advance.

After this brief conversation, the broker and purchaser turned to other matters:

Broker: Anything else you got a question about?

Purchaser: I don't understand the homeowners' association, this thing I have to pay forty-five dollars a month to. What do they do?

Broker: They have a kitty, and you put money into it. And you're a member of it. You elect officers among themselves, and they spend the money. Their function is to hold meetings, et cetera, and take care of the common areas, and do certain other things. For instance, if one of your neighbors is leaving trash around, you can go to them. Sort of like an in-house police force.

Purchaser: What do they support or pay for?

Broker: The outside grass strip next to the street, for one thing; they maintain that.

Purchaser: Are the officers of the association paid?

Broker: Not usually.

There followed discussions about warranties on appliances, air conditioning and heating equipment (a federal law requires these to be delivered in the sale of a new home, but difficulties had followed from the fact that the builder had had financial trouble, and certain warranties were still missing), about termite and foundation inspections, and about similar matters.

At approximately 2:45, the receptionist notified the purchaser and broker that the closer would see them in her office. She was running fifteen minutes behind schedule because another closing had taken longer than expected.

DISCUSSIONS WITH THE ESCROW AGENT

The closer looked at the escrow agreement that the parties had drawn up. It read as follows:

"A sum of $350.00 is to be placed in an escrow account for up to a 30 day period to cover costs of the items to be completed: touch up paint in various rooms, clean off spattered paint off cabinets, walls and floors, repair lock on upstairs door, paint front door, clean up trash in house and yard, mow grass in rear patio yard, touch up finish on kitchen cabinets."

She refused to accept the duty to serve as escrow agent under the terms of this agreement, and the following conversation occurred:

Title company closer: This escrow agreement isn't specific enough. (To broker): If he contracts for repairs and it's more than $350, what do I do with the $350?

Broker: Well, they did it like that on another transaction.

Closer: That's not our policy. I have to be very specific about escrow agreements. (To purchaser): Would you be willing to accept whatever repairs can be done for $350? And if the work isn't done completely, you get what's left of the $350?

The purchaser had already determined that the repairs were minor, and he did not wish to delay the closing on account of the risk that they might not be done. He answered, "Yes."

It was then necessary to obtain the agreement of the seller to this arrangement. The closer had to contact the responsible official at the bank, explain the problem, and obtain his agreement over the telephone.

Closer: And it's okay with you that he gets the money if the repairs aren't done?

Seller: Yes.

Closer: And as the matter is done, you submit bills to me and I'll pay them, then refund the remainder if they're completed in thirty days?

Seller: Yes.

These and other conversations ultimately resulted in a new escrow agreement, providing better guidance as to the duties of the title company and stating that the title company would be held harmless except as escrow agent. The agreement, drawn up by the parties and closer, follows.

SPECIAL ESCROW AGREEMENT

June 30, 2014

TO: WEST YORK TITLE COMPANY

A sum of $350.00 is to be placed in an escrow account with West York Title Company as escrow agent for up to a 30 day period to cover cost of the items to be completed.

1. Touch up paint in various rooms.
2. Build clothes support bracket in master bedroom closet.
3. Clean off splattered paint off cabinets, walls and floors.
4. Repair lock on upstairs door.
5. Paint front door.
6. Clean up trash in house and yard.
7. Mow grass in rear patio yard.
8. Touch up finish on kitchen cabinets.
9. Disposal Repair.

It is agreed that this account is to be disbursed to agents of seller only for actual, reasonable costs of work done after the day of closing. No charges against the fund can be made for earlier repairs or for items other than those listed. Seller agrees to complete such repairs within 30 days and submit bills for these repairs. If repairs are not completed within 30 days the Title Company will pay bills submitted up to that time and disburse the remaining funds to Edgar Pynes.

West York Title Company will be held harmless as to performance or non-performance of this agreement other than as escrow agent.

Very truly yours,

By: _Michael E. Way_   _Edgar E. Pynes_

PARK BANK

NOTE ON THE ROLE OF AN ATTORNEY AT CLOSING

As you may have surmised, the broker is acting as a surrogate for an attorney in some respects here. Whether that role is a desirable one is a matter of judgment. Whether the advice he gives is fully accurate is also an open question (is the homeowner's association really like an "in-house police force?"), but his explanation is probably more useful and understandable than one that might be more detailed and comprehensive.

An attorney at a closing might play a variety of roles. In States in which it is customary for attorneys' offices to be the place for residential closings, attorneys often perform escrow functions in addition to other duties, for example. In larger transactions, attorneys may serve the not unimportant function of keeping all the documents straight and ensuring that the right ones are signed by the right people, representing their clients in resolving any disputes that remain, and (in extreme cases) advising their clients whether to discontinue the closing. (Or, if the closing presents no difficulties, an attorney may find himself superfluous except as moral support to his client.)

NOTE ON MORE COMPLEX TRANSACTIONS

How would the closing of a more complex transaction differ from this one? Again, it would in many respects be analogous. The solution of problems by escrow arrangements would characterize the transaction, for example.

Ironically, the commerical transaction would not require some of the documents that appear in this chapter (in particular, federally imposed disclosure requirements, designed to protect consumers, would be fewer). The documents central to the transaction, however, would be both more numerous and more complex, as you might expect. The transfer of recently constructed income-producing property, for example, might well involve separate instruments transferring various property other than the realty (personalty, deposits, accounts receivable, etc.), dealing with construction liens or other encumbrances, and ensuring performance by bonds or other means.

C. EXECUTION OF THE CORE DOCUMENTS, DELIVERY OF THE DEED, AND ISSUANCE OF THE TITLE POLICY

The core documents and title insurance have been dealt with in previous chapters, but it should be remembered that the closing is the occasion for their execution. The deed is delivered in the manner described in the attorney's instructions to the closer. The title policy is customarily sent to the purchaser by mail, and a mortgagee policy (insuring the lender's interest) is simultaneously issued.

D. EXCERPTS FROM CLOSING DOCUMENTS: UNDERTAKINGS OR AUTHORIZATIONS BY BUYER

AUTHORIZATION TO PAY MORTGAGE INSURANCE PREMIUM

AUTHORIZATION TO PAY MORTGAGE INSURANCE PREMIUM

For valuable consideration, the undersigned agreed that _____*Huntington Savings Association*_____, mortgagee, may, at any time during the mortgage term, and at its discretion, apply for renewal of mortgage loan insurance covering the mortgage executed by the undersigned on even date herewith, pay the premium due by reason thereof, and require repayment by the undersigned of such amounts as are advanced by said mortgagee. In the event of failure by the undersigned to repay said amounts to said mortgagee, such failure shall be considered a default, and all provisions of the note and mortgage with regard to default shall be applicable.

Dated this ____*30*____ day of ____*June*_____, 2014.

Edgar E. Rynes
Andrew B. Rynes

AFFIDAVIT FOR FNMA/FHMLC COMPLIANCE

FEDERAL NATIONAL MORTGAGE ASSOCIATION
AFFIDAVIT OF PURCHASER AND VENDOR

I. PARTIES: (Name and address)

Lender ___ HUNTINGTON SAVINGS ASSOCIATION ___
___ 2530 WINSTON, LONDON, WEST YORK 77063 ___

Mortgage Insurer ___
(If applicable)

Property Vendor ___ PARK BANK OF LONDON ___

Property Purchaser ___ EDGAR E. PYNES AND ANDREW B. PYNES ___

II. PROPERTY ADDRESS OR LEGAL DESCRIPTION: (Attach supplemental sheet if necessary) ___

7947 BRAINERD LANE, LONDON, WEST YORK 77040

III. THE PURPOSE OF THE LOAN ON THIS PROPERTY IS:

☒ To purchase it from the above vendors — Total Purchase Price . . . . $ _834,200_

☐ To refinance outstanding debt.

☐ Other (Explain)

IV. FINANCIAL TERMS:

First Mortgage Amount . . . . $ _600,000_

Cash Equity (Not necessary for refinance) . . . . _234,200_

Secondary Financing:

Amount . . . . ___

Interest Rate ___ % Term ___
(Mos)

Monthly Payment $

Name and Address of Holder:

___
___

Other (Explain) ___

Total Purchase Price (Not necessary for refinance) . . . . $ _834,200_

V. LIENS: If this loan exceeds 80% of the appraised value or the purchase price of the property described in Item II above, no lien or charge upon such property has been given or executed or has been contracted or agreed to be so given or executed by Property Purchaser to any person, including Property Vendor, except for (1) liens disclosed in Item IV hereof, or (2) liens or charges which will be discharged from the proceeds of the subject mortgage.

VI. OCCUPANCY: Purchaser is now actually occupying the property described in Item II above or in good faith intends to so occupy such property as the principal residence.

VII. INDUCEMENT: The certifications of this Affidavit are for the purpose of inducing the Lender named above or its assignees to make or purchase the first mortgage described by this Affidavit, and inducing the Mortgage Insurer, if any, to insure such loan. Those executing this Affidavit acknowledge that if this loan exceeds 80% of the value or purchase price of the property and is made by a Federal Savings and Loan Association, and/or is subsequently purchased by a Federal Savings and Loan Association, the certifications of this Affidavit shall be used for the purpose of inducing a Federal Savings and Loan Association to enter into such transaction and that the provisions of Section 1014 of Title 18, United States Code, which provide in part "Whoever knowingly makes any false statement or report for the purpose of influencing in any way the action of . . . a Federal Savings and Loan Association . . . upon any application . . . shall be fined not more than $5,000 or imprisoned not more than two years or both," are applicable to such transaction.

VIII. PROPERTY VENDOR: The PROPERTY VENDOR hereby certifies that, to the extent PROPERTY VENDOR is a party, the Financial Terms, including Total Purchase Price, and the Liens are as set forth in Items III and IV above, hereby acknowledges the inducement purpose of this Affidavit as set forth in Item VII above, and certifies that certain of the prepaid expenses involved in the transaction (i.e., interest charges, real estate taxes, hazard insurance premiums, and private mortgage insurance renewal premiums) have not been paid by the vendor on behalf of the property purchaser.

Sworn to and subscribed before me

[This document is designed to enhance the function of FNMA and FHLMC in increasing residential ownership and availability. The remainder of the document is omitted.]

UCC-1 FINANCING STATEMENT COVERING PERSONALTY

Uniform Commercial Code—FINANCING STATEMENT—Form UCC-1

Filing Fee $ 5.00   IMPORTANT   Read instructions on back before filling out form

3. For Filing Officer (Date, Time, Number and Filing Office)

1. Debtor(s) Name and Mailing Address:
(Do not abbreviate)

Record Owners:
**Edgar Pynes and
Andrew B. Pynes,**
7947 Brainerd Lane
London, W.Y. 77040

2. Secured Party(ies) Name and Address:

HUNTINGTON SAVINGS
Association
P. O. Box 6981
2530 Winston
London, W.Y. 77002

5. Name and Address of Assignee of Secured Party: (Use this space to describe collateral, if needed)

4. This Financing Statement covers the following types (or items) of property:
(If collateral is crops, fixtures, timber or minerals, read instructions on back.)

All air conditioning, plumbing and heating equipment, ranges, dishwashers, water heaters, garbage disposal units, and all additions, accessions and substitutions thereto or therefor, now or hereafter attached to or located in or about the buildings erected or to be erected. The above goods are, or are to become fixtures on: Lot 65, Block 2, LEEBROOK TOWN HOUSE SUBDIVISION, Harris County, Texas, according to map or plat thereof, recorded in Volume 203, Page 87, Map Records, Manero County, West York (SEE ATTACHED DESCRIPTION).

Check only if applicable
X This Financing Statement is to be filed for record in the real estate records.   [ ] Products of collateral are also covered.

Number of additional sheets presented __1__

5. This Statement is signed by the Secured Party instead of the Debtor to perfect a security interest in collateral
(Please check) [ ] already subject to a security interest in another jurisdiction when it was brought into this state, or when the debtor's location was changed to this state, or
appropriate box)
[ ] already subject to a financing statement filed in another county.
[ ] which is proceeds of the original collateral described above in which a security interest was perfected, or
[ ] as to which the filing has lapsed, or
[ ] acquired after a change of name, identity or corporate structure of the debtor.

Edgar E. Pynes
Arthur Pynes

Use whichever signature line is applicable.

HUNTINGTON   SAVINGS ASSOCIATION
By *Michael F. Way*
Signature(s) of Secured Party(ies)

STANDARD FORM — FORM UCC-1 (REV. 6-19-75) APPROVED BY THE SECRETARY OF STATE OF TEXAS FORM 15 1549

AGREEMENT TO CORRECT POSSIBLE DOCUMENT ERRORS ("COMPLIANCE AGREEMENT")

Borrowers, in consideration of the Lender disbursing funds today for the closing of property located at 7947 Brainerd Lane, Houston, Texas 77040 ("Property") agree, if requested by Lender or someone acting on behalf of Lender, to cooperate and adjust for clerical errors any and all loan closing documents deemed necessary or desirable in the reasonable discretion of Lender to enable Lender to sell, convey, seek guaranty or market the Loan to any entity, including but not limited to an investor, Federal National Mortgage Association (FNMA), Government National Mortgage Association (GNMA), Federal Home Loan Mortgage Corporation, Department of Housing and Urban Development, Veterans Administration, or any Municipal Bonding Authority.

Borrowers agree to comply with all such requests from Lender within thirty (30) days from the date of mailing of such requests by Lender. Borrowers agree to assume all costs including, by way of illustration and not limitation, actual expenses, legal fees and marketing losses for failing to comply with Lender's requests within such thirty (30) day period.

Borrowers do hereby so agree and covenant in order to assure that the loan documents executed this date will conform with and be acceptable in the market place in the instance of transfer, sale or conveyance by Lender of its interest in and to the Loan.

[Execution, by purchasers, omitted here.]

72

E. EXCERPTS FROM CLOSING DOCUMENTS: DISCLOSURES

ATTORNEY REPRESENTATION DISCLOSURE

I. STATUS OF CORTELLI & BARNES

Legal instruments and loan documentation involved in the above referenced loan and real property transaction have been prepared for Huntington Savings Association ("Lender") by the law firm of CORTELLI AND BARNES, P.C., Attorneys and Counselors (" C&B "). The undersigned acknowledge that C&B has acted only as counsel to the Lender, and has not, in any manner, undertaken to assist or render legal advice to the undersigned, or either of them, with respect to the loan or the purchase (or sale) of the real property described in the above referenced loan, or with respect to any of the documents or instruments being executed in connection therewith. The undersigned further acknowledge that they are aware that they are free to retain their own counsel to advise them regarding the loan or purchase (or sale) of the real property, or to review and render advice concerning any of the documents or instruments being executed in connection therewith.

II. BORROWER'S RESPONSIBILITY FOR PAYMENT OF FEES

Borrower and Seller acknowledge Borrower's obligation to fulfill its agreement with the Lender to pay the legal fees of the Lender incurred in connection with the preparation of legal instruments and loan documentation by making, at the loan closing, a payment in the amount set forth in Paragraph IV directly to C&B for the account of Lender.

III. DESCRIPTION OF LEGAL SERVICES PERFORMED

In connection with the preparation of the legal instruments and loan documentation, an examination was made of the executed purchase agreement to verify that the same is in conformity with the commitment to lend as issued by the Lender. Also, a review was made of the Commitment for Title Insurance to determine its acceptability to the Lender as to any exceptions to be noted on the final Title Insurance Policy. The file was noted and checked to determine whether the property has been cleared of all encumbrances and liens which are objectionable to the Lender. A review was made of the Survey to determine whether it conforms with the legal description of the property, to determine whether the improvements located on the surrounding properties encroach on the subject property or to determine whether it conforms to the Commitment for Title Insurance. The documentation which has been prepared included one or more of the following: the Note, Deed of Trust, any required Riders, Warranty Deed, associated mortgage insurance and tax information documentation and certain affidavits required by the Lender.

IV. BASIS FOR FEE AND AMOUNT OF FEE

The fee is intended to provide fair compensation for the above described services taking into consideration the time and labor required, the complexities of the questions involved and the skill required to perform said services. Other considerations include the expertise of C & B in the complexities of the real estate practice, the necessary overhead associated with the rendering of the said services and the assumption of risk by the firm in the rendering of said services. The fee established for the above described legal services is $ 250.00 . This amount does not include a charge for preparation of the Truth in Lending Disclosure Statement.

Each Borrower and Seller hereby acknowledges receiving and reading a copy of this statement, and by his/her signature affirm his/her acknowledgement of the accuracy of the statements contained in Paragraphs I and II above.

SELLER:
Park Bank of London
by: Michael E. Way, V. Pres.

BORROWER:
Edgar E. Pynee
Andrew B Pynee

OMB No. 2502-0265

A. Settlement Statement (HUD-1)

B. Type of Loan

1. ☐ FHA 2. ☐ RHS 3. ☒ Conv Unins 4. ☐ VA 5. ☐ Conv Ins. 6. ☐ Seller Fin 7. ☐ Cash Sale.	6. File Number 2647000580 7. Loan Number 5110000045 8. Mortgage Ins Case Number

C. Note: This form is furnished to give you a statement of actual settlement costs. Amounts paid to and by the settlement agent are shown. Items marked "(p.o.c.)" were paid outside the closing; they are shown here for informational purposes and are not included in the totals.

D. Name & Address of Borrower	E. Name & Address of Seller	F. Name & Address of Lender
Edgar Pynes and Andrew Pynes 43A Sandra St. London, West York 77040	Park Bank Park Bank Building London, West York 77040	Huntington Savings Association Huntington Savings Building London, West York 77040

G. Property Location	H. Settlement Agent Name	I. Settlement Date
Lot 65, Block 2, Texas Leebrook Town House Subdivision, Manero County, West York 7947 Brainerd Lane 77040	West York Title Insurance Company 1332 Main Street London, West York 77002 .derwritten By: Commonwealth	
	Place of Settlement West York Title Insurance Company 1332 Main Street London, West York 77002	

J. Summary of Borrower's Transaction		K. Summary of Seller's Transaction	
100. Gross Amount Due from Borrower		**400. Gross Amount Due to Seller**	
101. Contract sales price	$834,200.00	401. Contract sales price	$834,200.00
102. Personal property		402. Personal property	
103. Settlement charges to borrower	$17,628.66	403.	
104.		404.	
105.		405.	
Adjustments for items paid by seller in advance		**Adjustments for items paid by seller in advance**	
106. City property taxes		406. City property taxes	
107. County property taxes		407. County property taxes	
108. Annual assessments		408. Annual assessments	
109. School property taxes		409. School property taxes	
110. MUD taxes		410. MUD taxes	
111. Other		411. Other	
112.		412.	
113.		413.	
114.		414.	
115.		415.	
116.		416.	
120. Gross Amount Due From Borrower	$851,828.66	**420. Gross Amount Due to Seller**	$834,200.00
200. Amounts Paid By Or In Behalf Of Borrower		**500. Reductions In Amount Due to Seller**	
201. Deposit or earnest money	$8,000.00	501. Excess deposit (see instructions)	
202. Principal amount of new loan(s)	$600,000.00	502. Settlement charges to seller (line 1400)	$17,418.58
203. Existing loan(s) taken subject to		503. Existing loan(s) taken subject to	
204.		504. Payoff of first mortgage loan	$745,625.18
205.		505. Payoff of second mortgage loan	
206. Option Fee	$100.00	506. Option Fee	$100.00
207.		507. (EMD $8,000 Disbursed as Proceeds)	
208. Portion of Owner's Policy Paid by Seller	$4,769.00	508. Portion of Owner's Policy Paid by Seller	$4,769.00
209.		509.	
Adjustments for items unpaid by seller		**Adjustments for items unpaid by seller**	
210. City property taxes 01/01/11 thru 03/14/11	$629.88	510. City property taxes 01/01/11 thru 03/14/11	$629.88
211. County property taxes 01/01/11 thru 03/14/11	$1,147.89	511. County property taxes 01/01/11 thru 03/14/11	$1,147.89
212. Annual assessments		512. Annual assessments	
213. School property taxes 01/01/11 thru 03/14/11	$1,821.90	513. School property taxes 01/01/11 thru 03/14/11	$1,821.90
214. MUD taxes		514. MUD taxes	
215. Other		515. Other	
216.		516.	
217.		517.	
218.		518.	
219.		519.	
220. Total Paid By/For Borrower	$616,468.67	**520. Total Reduction Amount Due Seller**	$771,512.43
300. Cash At Settlement From/To Borrower		**600. Cash At Settlement To/From Seller**	
301. Gross Amount due from borrower (line 120)	$851,828.66	601. Gross Amount due to seller (line 420)	$834,200.00
302. Less amounts paid by/for borrower (line 220)	$616,468.67	602. Less reductions in amt. due seller (line 520)	$771,512.43
303. Cash From Borrower	$235,359.99	603. Cash To Seller	$62,687.57

The Public Reporting Burden for this collection of information is estimated at 35 minutes per response for collecting, reviewing, and reporting the data. This agency may not collect this information, and you are not required to complete this form, unless it displays a currently valid OMB control number. No confidentiality is assured; this disclosure is mandatory. This is designed to provide the parties to a RESPA covered transaction with information during the settlement process.

L. Settlement Charges

700. Total Real Estate Broker Fees			$17,200.00			Paid From Borrower's Funds at Settlement	Paid From Seller's Funds at Settlement
Division of Commission (line 700) as follows:							
701. $17,200.00		to	Betty K. Morris				
702.		to					
703. Commission Paid at Settlement						$0.00	$17,200.00
704. The following persons, firms or corporations received a porton of the real		to					
705. estate commission amount shown above:		to					

800. Items Payable in Connection with Loan							
801. Our origination charge				$1,250.00	(from GFE #1)		
802. Your credit or charge (points) for the specific rate chosen				$0.00	(from GFE #2)		
803. Your adjusted origination charges		to			(from GFE A)	$1,250.00	
804. Appraisal Fee		to	LSI	POC (B) $600.00	(from GFE #3)	$-155.00	
805. Credit report		to	CoreLogic Credco	POC (B) $35.00	(from GFE #3)	$-5.63	
806. Tax service		to	Dovenmuehle		(from GFE #3)	$83.00	
807. Flood certification		to	Corelogic Flood Services		(from GFE #3)	$15.00	
808. Attorney Review		to	Brown, Fowler & Alsup		$125.00 (from GFE #1)		$0.00

900. Items Required by Lender To Be Paid in Advance							
901. Daily interest charges from 3/14/2011 to 4/1/2011 @ $70.8333/day					(from GFE #10)	$1,275.00	
902. Mortgage Insurance Premium for months		to			(from GFE #3)		
903. Homeowner's insurance for 1 years		to	Fireman's Fund Insurance Company		(from GFE #11)	$1,643.00	

1000. Reserves Deposited With Lender							
1001. Initial Deposit for your escrow account					(from GFE #9)	$8,177.64	
1002. Homeowner's insurance	3	months @	$136.92	per month	$410.76		
1003. Mortgage insurance		months @	$0.00	per month	$0.00		
1004. City property taxes		months @		per month	$0.00		
1005. County property taxes	6	months @	$1,499.86	per month	$8,999.16		
1006. Annual assessments		months @		per month	$0.00		
1007. School property taxes		months @		per month	$0.00		
1008. MUD taxes		months @		per month	$0.00		
1009. Other	0	months @					
1010. Flood Insurance	0	months @					
1011. Aggregate Adjustment					$-1,232.28		

1100. Title Charges							
1101. Title services and lender's title insurance		to			(from GFE #4)	$440.65	
1102. Settlement or closing fee		to					
1103. Owner's title insurance		to			(from GFE #5)	$4,769.00	
1104. Lender's title insurance		to				$395.65	
1105. Lender's title policy limit $		$600,000.00/$395.65 .					
1106. Owner's title policy limit $		$834,200.00/$4,764.00					
1107. Agent's portion of the total title insurance premium		to		$4,385.70			
1108. Underwriter's portion of the total title insurance premium		to		$773.95			
1109. State Policy Guaranty Fee		to	Title Insurance Guaranty Association	$5.00 (from GFE #4)			$0.00
1110. State Policy Guaranty Fee		to	Title Insurance Guaranty Association	$5.00 (from GFE #5)			$0.00
1111.		to					
1112. E File Fee		to			(from GFE #4)		$0.00
1113. Messenger Fee		to	Commonwealth Title of Houston	$40.00 (from GFE #4)			$15.00
1114. Tax Certificates		to	National TaxNet				$71.58
1115. Document Preparation		to					$100.00

1200. Government Recording and Transfer Charges							
1201. Government recording charges					(from GFE #7)	$136.00	
1202. Deed $24.00 ; Mortgage $112.00 , Release $32.00		to	Commonwealth Title of Houston				$32.00
1203. Transfer taxes					(from GFE #8)		
1204. City/County tax/stamps	Deed $0.00 ; Mortgage $0.00						
1205. State tax/stamps	Deed $0.00 ; Mortgage $0.00						

1300. Additional Settlement Charges							
1301. Required services you can shop for					(from GFE #6)		

1400. Total Settlement Charges (enter on lines 103, Section J and 502, Section K)						$17,628.66	$17,418.58

POC (B) – Paid Outside of Closing by Borrower. POC (S) – Paid Outside of Closing by Seller. POC (L) – Paid Outside of Closing by Lender.

[Other parts of the document, including comparison of the good faith estimate to the actual charges, Charges that can still change, repeated loan terms, and signature of parties, are omitted here.]

REGULATION Z ("TRUTH IN LENDING") DISCLOSURE STATEMENT

LOAN DISCLOSURE STATEMENT
HUNTINGTON SAVINGS ASSOCIATION

[ ] Initial disclosure estimated at time of application. All numerical disclosures except the late payment disclosure are estimates.

[X] Final disclosure based on closing terms. E Means estimate.

Date: 06/30/84	Borrower:	EDGAR E. PYNES AND ANDREW B. PYNES	
Loan #: 2000001	Property:	7947 BRAINERD LANE, LONDON, WEST YORK 77040	

Loan Number: 00005110000045   **Date: 02/10/2011**

ANNUAL PERCENTAGE RATE	FINANCE CHARGE	Amount Financed	Total of Payments
The cost of your credit as a yearly rate.	The dollar amount the credit will cost you.	The amount of credit provided to you or on your behalf.	The amount you will have paid after you have made all payments as scheduled.
3.5295%	$439,754.86	$664,535.20	$1,104,290.06

INTEREST RATE AND PAYMENT SUMMARY

	INTRODUCTORY Rate & Monthly Payment (for first 60 months)	MAXIMUM During FIRST FIVE YEARS April 01, 2016	MAXIMUM EVER (as early as April 01, 2018)
Interest Rate	4.2500 %	6.2500 %	9.2500 %
Principal Payment	-None-	$926.54	$680.64
Interest Payment	$2,363.57	$3,475.83	$4,986.08
Estimate Taxes + Insurance (Escrow) ☐ Includes Private Mortgage Insurance ☐ Includes Mortgage Insurance	$1,828.17	$1,828.17	$1,828.17
Total Estimated Monthly Payment	$4,191.74	$6,230.54	$7,494.89

☐ **Introductory Rate Notice.**
You have a discounted introductory rate of   % that ends after
In the   even if market rates do not change, this rate will increase to   %.

VARIABLE RATE: Your loan contains a variable-rate feature. Disclosures about the variable-rate feature have been provided to you earlier.

INSURANCE: The following insurance is required to obtain credit: *Property
You may obtain the insurance from anyone that is acceptable to creditor.

SECURITY: You are giving a security interest in the real property being purchased.
Property address: 4914 TAMARISK ST, BELLAIRE, TX 77401

LATE CHARGE: If a payment is more than 15 days late, you will be charged 5.0000% of the payment, not less than $25.00.

PREPAYMENT: If you pay off your loan early, * You will not have to pay a penalty.
* You will not be entitled to a refund of part of the finance charge.

ASSUMPTION: Someone buying your property cannot assume the remainder of your loan on the original terms.

NO GUARANTEE TO REFINANCE: There is no guarantee that you will be able to refinance to lower your rate and payments.

All dates and numerical disclosures except the late payment disclosure are estimates.

See your contract documents for any additional information about nonpayment, default, any required repayment in full before the scheduled date, and prepayment refunds and penalties.

You are not required to complete this agreement merely because you have received these disclosures or signed a loan application.

Edgar E. Pynes
_____ DATE
Andrew B. Pynes
_____ DATE

NOTE ON OTHER CLOSING DOCUMENTS

The closing may (and typically does) involve many documents in addition to those illustrated here. State law may require further disclosures (in some States, for example, the lender or seller must provide detailed information about the taxing authorities having jurisdiction over the property). The buyer may be required to acknowledge his acceptance of certain aspects of the transaction, such as the estimates of taxes for the current year that are used to prorate taxes or the exceptions in the title policy. There may be conveyances of personalty by the seller to the buyer (as, for example, with appliances, if they are transferred; there would be a bill of sale in such an instance, which fulfills much the same function as the deed). The point is that the documents reproduced here are illustrative of common or uniformly required ones, and the nature and number of other documents varies with the contours of the transaction.

F. NOTES AND QUESTIONS ON THE CLOSING

1. THE PLACE THE CLOSING OCCUPIES IN THE TRANSACTION. The closing is the consummation of the transaction, but in a sense it is an anticlimax. In many cases it is a mechanical process of executing documents prepared as a result of the contract of purchase and sale. On the other hand, the closing can be the occasion for resolving serious and lingering disputes. In such instances, the closing can be an acrimonious, adversarial process rather than a mechanical one.

2. THE USE OF ESCROW ARRANGEMENTS IN RESOLVING DISPUTES. This transaction gives a hint of the way in which disputes can arise and be resolved at a closing. An issue that could have been solved earlier still remains. Human nature, time pressures, and the contingent nature of scheduled closings contribute to make this situation a common one in some kinds of transactions (it is more common in commercial transactions than residential ones, although it occurs there also). The use of an escrow account can allow the dispute to be resolved in a way that preserves obligations but does not delay the closing. At its simplest, an escrow arrangement involves a stakeholder who is to pay funds upon the occurrence of a specified event.

3. THE DISADVANTAGES OF ESCROWS. The escrow agent is wise to remember that it is literally standing between two disputing parties. Despite our preference not to be "caught in the middle," that is precisely the position the escrow agent undertakes. Does this position explain the title insurer's concern about the specificity of the escrow agreement? An unclear agreement can cause cost and delay for all three parties. The title insurer, however, is willing to undertake the obligation here because it has time and effort invested in the closing, just as the other parties do. Another example of an escrow is the account for taxes and insurance that is maintained by the lender (in which there is no third party, but the lender occupies two roles). In the purchase and sale of an apartment complex, escrows may be maintained for repairs, taxes, contingent liabilities, and other purposes, which may be analogous to the purpose of the escrow here.

4. THE BUYER-BORROWER'S UNDERTAKINGS. The Affidavit of Buyer and Seller is required for a FNMA-FHLMC loan since these organizations were chartered to support residential home ownership. Private mortgage insurance ("PMI") is insurance against an uncollectable deficiency in the event of default. If there is a larger down payment, PMI may not be required; usually Lender requires it because down payment is only 5% of the purchase price.

5. PRIVATELY VOLUNTEERED DISCLOSURES. Why does the lender's attorney so carefully document the buyer's awareness that he is not the buyer's attorney? (Hint: if, as is common in some States, the lender's attorney prepares the deed, and if the deed excepts more broadly than a buyer might prefer, and if this drafting causes the buyer to obtain a lesser interest than he expects, might the buyer take action against the attorney? Indeed, might the buyer argue that he was misled into believing that an attorney was protecting his interests since he paid the fee, and thus attribute to the attorney all manner of

losses?)

6. LEGALLY REQUIRED DISCLOSURES. The Buyer's Statement and Seller's Statement are portions of a form promulgated by the Department of Housing and Urban Development, pursuant to the Real Estate Settlement Procedures Act ("RESPA"). Together with the "Good Faith Estimate of Settlement Charges" seen in an earlier chapter (as well as other processes), this document is part of an effort to ensure consumer awareness as a means of preventing abuses. The document is in a uniform national form, designed to be readily comprehensible to unsophisticated buyers and sellers.

7. THE REGULATION Z ("TRUTH-IN-LENDING") STATEMENT. The "Annual Percentage Rate" is a single figure that is designed to summarize the cost of the loan so as to enable the borrower to shop for credit. It incorporates not only the interest rate and other terms of the loan affecting the cost of credit, but also the "points" and other "front-end" charges (and takes account of the fact they are paid in advance). It also tells the buyer the total cost of his credit over the life of the loan (this figure is at the same time both interesting because it is larger than the amount of the loan and relatively useless because a loan with a larger absolute cost of credit may be preferable to a loan with a smaller one—if, for example, the smaller one entails a shorter term). One may question the efficacy of these disclosures in any event.

8. THE COSTS AND BENEFITS OF DISCLOSURE. Businesspeople often dislike disclosure requirements because they create unknown liabilities. For example, failure to comply with the Truth in Lending Act can create liabilities disproportionate to resulting harm, and good faith error is not generally a defense. The difficulty of computing the components of disclosure forms should not be underestimated (the authors obtained differing amounts from different service providers on several components for this very transaction). The lender is thus motivated to expend effort disproportionate to the value of the information to ensure its protection, and this effort is itself reflected in increased cost of the loan. On the other hand, imposition of arbitrary settlement charges in large amounts was one of the abuses to which these laws were directed. What is the proper level of required disclosure?

9. CLOSING INSTRUCTIONS. Notice the detail of the closing instructions written by the lender's attorney. Why is it necessary to instruct the title company to see that each document is signed and dated? Wouldn't any intelligent person know to do that? (Hint: notice that the instructions include return of a signed copy of the instructions themselves, expressly constituting a warranty that the instructions were complied with.)

G. RECORDING AND DELIVERY

COUNTY CLERK'S FILE STAMP ON DEED

FILED
JUL 21 9:47 AM
AMANDA SCHNEAR
COUNTY CLERK
MANERO COUNTY, WEST YORK
BY: _Paul Bates_
DEPUTY

COUNTY CLERK'S INDEXING STAMP ON DEED

INDEXED
E197979
168-20
AMANDA SCHNEAR
COUNTY CLERK
MANERO COUNTY, WEST YORK
BY: _Paul Bates_
DEPUTY

EXCERPT FROM GRANTOR-GRANTEE INDEX

DIRECT MASTER INDEX TO REAL PROPERTY RECORDS

AL ATTACHMENT LIEN	EM MECHANIC'S AND MATERIALMAN'S LIEN	IA ALIEN OWNERSHIP OF LAND	MM MORTGAGE	SL STATE TAX LIEN
BS BILL OF SALE	FL FEDERAL LIEN	JJ JUDGEMENT	NS PUBLIC SCHOOL LAND	TR TAX RECEIPT
CC CONTRACT	GB BOND TO PAY LIEN OR CLAIMS	LP LIMITED PARTNERSHIP	OM MAPS	XE SMALL ESTATE
DD DEED	HL LANDLORD LIEN	LR REAL PROPERTY LIEN	PP LIS PENDENS	YC CONDOMINIUM

| OR | EE | | | | | | RPI | | 289-18-4129 |

GRANTOR, MORTGAGOR, ASSIGNOR, PLAINTIFF, DEBTOR LIEN HOLDER, GENERAL PARTNER LANDLORD TAX PAYER, SELLER	GRANTEE, MORTGAGEE, ASSIGNEE, DEFENDANT CREDITOR, LIMITED PARTNER, TENANT TAX AGENCY, BUYER	KIND OF INSTRUMENT	R E C	VOL.	PAGE	FILM CODE	DATE FILED MO DAY YEAR	DESCRIPTION
***		FI STM	MM			166-18-1169	06-06	HARDIN W A24 0.097
PARK BANK LONDON	ALEXANDER O	A/J	JJ			167-15-0966	06-15	DKT 297368
PARK BANK LONDON	BULLARD LEE E	A/J	JJ			167-15-0968	06-15	DKT 288764
PARK BANK LONDON	NORTHOL MILES F ETAL NORTHOL ANN M ETAL	REL REL REL	MM MM MM			167-15-1278 167-15-1278 167-15-1278	06-15 06-15 06-15	SUBURBIA L4 CLAY A LD PT/LT EWING A A245 09652
PARK BANK LONDON	GULF COAST ATHLETIC CI ETA LUMLEY EDWARD RAY ETAL LUMLEY NAOMI R ETAL	A/J	JJ			167-20-1383	06-17	DKT 1126445
PARK BANK LONDON	APOGEE INC	W/D W/D W/D	DD DD DD			168-03-0322 168-03-0322 168-03-0322	06-20 06-20 06-20	HABERMACHER S A331 P44.9 WHEELER T K A826 P44.9 LEWIS A A506 P44.9
PARK BANK LONDON	DREW MTG CO	ASSGN ASSGN ASSGN	DD DD DD			168-03-0322 168-03-0322 168-03-0322	06-20 06-20 06-20	HABERMACHER S A331 P44.9 WHEELER T K A826 P44.9 LEWIS A A506 P44.9
PARK BANK LONDON	FAIRFIELD CO INC	PT REL PT REL	DD DD			168-07-0390 168-07-0390	06-22 06-22	HARDIN W A24 0.135 STONEHENGE RC B2 P/RES
PARK BANK LONDON	KOSSOW BLDR INC	FI STM FI STM	MM MM			168-07-0393 168-07-0393	06-22 06-22	HARDIN W A24 0.135 STONEHENGE RC B2 P/RES
PARK BANK LONDON	MULLAN JERRY ALLEN ETAL MULLAN GLENDA RAYE ETAL	W/D	DD			168-11-0251	06-24	LINCOLN PARK FMS BE PT/BL
PARK BANK LONDON	BOLAN GARY O ETAL GLOWB LAND CO INC ETAL	A/J	JJ			168-12-0853	06-24	DKT 1108444
PARK BANK LONDON	CAMCO CONST CORP	PT REL PT REL	MM MM			168-14-1846 168-14-1846	06-27 06-27	COMPOUND THE INSTR WESTHEIMER ESTS L54 PT/LT
PARK BANK LONDON	CAMCO CONST CORP	FI STM FI STM	MM MM			168-14-1849 168-14-1849	06-27 06-27	COMPOUND THE INSTR WESTHEIMER ESTS L54
PARK BANK LONDON	CAMCO CONST CORP	FI STM FI STM	MM MM			168-14-1852 168-14-1852	06-27 06-27	COMPOUND THE INSTR WESTHEIMER ESTS L54
PARK BANK LONDON	ROY F JOHNSON BLDR INC	FI STM	MM			168-17-0671	06-28	SPRING SHDWS 17 L11 BW50
PARK BANK LONDON	PYNES EDGAR E PYNES ANDREW B ET AL	W/D	DD			168-20-1894	07-21	LEEBROOK TWNHSE L65 B2
PARK BANK LONDON	ALLEY CHARLES Y	A/J	JJ			169-02-2486	07-01	DKT 846324A
PARK BANK LONDON	ILFORD D SHERMER ETAL TIMES WALLY X ETAL GRIPP ROBERT A ETAL	REL REL	CC CC			169-12-2286 169-12-2286	07-08 07-08	SYLVAN BEACH #1 L1 B18 HUNTER J
PARK BANK LONDON	91 SPRING BR INC	PT REL	MM			169-12-2537	07-08	SPRING BR VAL L12 BL

79

EXCERPT FROM REVERSE (GRANTEE-GRANTOR) INDEX

REVERSE MASTER INDEX TO REAL PROPERTY RECORDS — MANERO COUNTY, W.Y.

GRANTEE, MORTGAGEE, ASSIGNEE, DEFENDANT, CREDITOR, LIMITED PARTNER, TENANT, TAX AGENCY, BUYER	GRANTOR, MORTGAGOR, ASSIGNOR, PLAINTIFF, DEBTOR, LIEN HOLDER, GENERAL PARTNER, LANDLORD, TAX PAYER, SELLER	TYPE OF INSTRUMENT	R/C	VOL	PAGE	FILM CODE	MO DAY YEAR	DESCRIPTION
PYNES HAROLD V ET AL	GENERAL HOMES INC ETAL / BLUME HAROLD VERNON ETAL	NOTICE	DD			164-19-1495	05-10	POSTWOOD 1 L5 B7
PYNES HAROLD VERNON	RICHARD BEACH CONST CO	W/D	DD			164-08-2493	05-03	CLEAR LK CY CORE M INSTR
PYNES IDA R ET AL	RICHARD BEACH CONST CO ETA / BLUME JACK S ETAL / BLUME IDA R ETAL	NOTICE	DD			164-08-2497	05-03	CLEAR LK CY CORE M INSTR
PYNES IDA R ET AL	BLUME JACK S ETAL / BLUME IDA R ETAL / RELOCATION RLTY SERV C ETA	NOTICE				138-96-2170	09-13	MIDDLEBROOK 2 L22 B39
PYNES IDA R	UNIVERSITY SAV ASSN	CINSTR				145-82-0979	11-28	SEE INSTR
PYNES IDA R	UNIVERSITY SAV ASSN	REL				146-91-1407	12-14	MIDDLEBROOK 2 L22 B39
PYNES JACK S	RICHARD BEACH CONST CO	W/D	DD			164-08-2493	05-03	MIDDLEBROOK 2 L22 B39
PYNES JACK S	RICHARD BEACH CONST CO ETA / BLUME JACK S ETAL / BLUME IDA R ETAL	NOTICE	DD			164-08-2497	05-03	CLEAR LK CY CORE M INSTR
PYNES JACK S	BLUME JACK S ETAL / BLUME IDA R ETAL / RELOCATION RLTY SERV C ETA	NOTICE				138-96-2170	09-13	MIDDLEBROOK 2 L22 B39
PYNES JACK S	UNIVERSITY SAV ASSN	CINSTR				145-82-0979	11-28	SEE INSTR
PYNES JACK S	UNIVERSITY SAV ASSN	REL				146-91-1407	12-14	MIDDLEBROOK 2 L22 B39
PYNES EDGAR E	PARK BANK LONDON	W/D	DD			168-20-1894	07-21	LEEBROOK TWNHSE L65 B2
PYNES JAMES	CENTRAL NATL BANK	FI STM				180-06-2292	11-11	NO 081301F
PYNES JAMES A	CONDON HOMES INC	W/D	DD			161-07-2279	03-22	PIFER GREEN L1
PYNES JAMES A	CENTRAL NATL BANK	REL				172-93-0761	12-01	PIFER GREEN L1
PYNES JAMES A	FIRST FED S&L AOM	CINSTR	DD			140-06-0728	05-03	SEE INSTR
PYNES JAMES ARN	EXXON CORP	REL				103-92-0485	08-16	SHERMAN PL L1 B2
PYNES JAMES L	TRAAS COMRC BANK-FW	A/J				163-88-1918	08-04	DKT 141-58380-79 T AR RANT C
PYNES JAMES M	LODGE JOHN H ETAL / LODGE MAGDALENA ETAL	W/D				105-82-2196	08-31	FALLBROOK 1 L128 B7
PYNES JANA M ETAL	LODGE JOHN H ETAL / LODGE MAGDALENA ETAL / CRANE LARRY W ETAL / CRANE JANA M ETAL	NOTICE				105-82-2199	08-31	FALLBROOK 1 L128 B7
PYNES JANE E ET AL	HALTER JOSEPH A ETAL	W/D				175-16-1060	09-19	WEST UNIV PL L2 B40 PT/LT

NOTE ON DELIVERY

Upon recording and payment of all fees, the escrow agent (West York Title Insurance Company) completed delivery of the deed and security instruments by mailing them together with a transmittal letter to the buyer and the lender, respectively.

H. PHOTOGRAPHS OF THE PROPERTY CONVEYED

LEEBROOK

SUBDIVISION

APPENDIX TO CHAPTER SIX:
HOW CLOSING DOCUMENTS SUCH AS THOSE IN THIS CHAPTER ARE PREPARED

A LAW FIRM FOR RESIDENTIAL LENDERS. The law firm of Cortelli and Barnes is located in a large midwestern city.

It has an interesting practice.

Cortelli and Barnes prepares residential loan documents for more than twenty different mortgage lenders, most of them large, multi-State operations. Its documents are used to close loans upon residences in Arizona, Arkansas, California, Colorado, Illinois, Louisiana, Minnesota, Texas, Wisconsin, and several other States.

Cortelli and Barnes has fifteen attorneys in its home office and seven in a neighboring State. But in addition to these twenty-two lawyers, Cortelli and Barnes has more than a hundred non-lawyer employees. The term "non-lawyer" may have a pejorative sound to most attorneys, but at Cortelli and Barnes, the non-lawyers are highly professional, important, and in many instances better paid than the average lawyer. They help Cortelli and Barnes carry on a highly efficient, valuable service. Although the firm conducts practice in several areas, including litigation and general representation of several publicly traded corporations, its mortgage lending practice makes it unique.

The documents in this chapter were prepared with the assistance of the lawyers and other professionals at Cortelli and Barnes, and the way in which they would be prepared by Cortelli and Barnes, if they were to be used in a real transaction, is fascinating.

STARTING THE PAPER FLOW: THE COMPUTER PREPARES THE INITIAL DISCLOSURE DOCUMENTS. The involvement of Cortelli and Barnes in a residential loan begins when one of its clients sends it a "Request for Preparation of Good Faith Estimate." The actual Request may have been prepared at a lender's branch office in Arizona or Wisconsin. A telecopier located at Cortelli and Barnes' offices produces a copy of the Request within seconds. It is handwritten or typed on a standard form by a distant loan officer after a home buyer's application, and it contains the information that Cortelli and Barnes will need to prepare the initial disclosure documents.

An operator at Cortelli and Barnes picks up the telecopy. He or she sits in front of a display screen and uses a keyboard to code the information into a computer. The computer is programmed to produce a RESPA Good Faith Estimate and a Regulation Z Disclosure Form, as well as a transmittal envelope with the borrower's address.

THE CLOSING DOCUMENTS. At a later date, the preparation of closing documents is initiated. The lender sends Cortelli and Barnes a one-page document entitled "Authorization to Close." It also furnishes a copy of the Title Commitment and the Contract of Purchase and Sale. The Authorization contains most of the information Cortelli and Barnes will need to prepare the closing documents; the commitment and contract are required primarily for the purpose of verifying that the transaction is lawful and that the security is properly protected.

The computer system is programmed to fill the blanks in the closing documents when it is instructed to do so.

"UNTOUCHED BY HUMAN HANDS:" THE STATE OF THE ART IN DOCUMENT PREPARATION. Cortelli and Barnes' computers are programmed so that they can produce documents for each State in which lenders represented by the firm are operating. Furthermore, the process is set up so that the computers can prepare documents for each different kind of loan that each lender might use: FHA,

VA or conventional; adjustable, graduated, or fixed; on FNMA forms, special secondary market forms, or custom forms. Once the parameters are entered into the computer, it takes over the task of preparing the papers.

At the time of this writing, the Cortelli and Barnes operator feeds the pre-printed papers through a printer, which is set up to fit the blanks that are to be filled in. Several walls of the office are covered with pigeonholes containing scores of different pre-printed forms, each carefully labelled. The process is rapid and efficient and reduces errors.

But Cortelli and Barnes is not satisfied with this hand-feed system. It can't afford to be, because it knows it must serve its clientele as well as the state of the art will allow.

And so Cortelli and Barnes is in the process of establishing a new procedure. The computer equipment will include a laser printer that can prepare a facsimile of a preprinted form at the same time that it fills in the blanks in the form. A sheet of paper will be continuously fed into the printer, and each of the documents necessary to a closing for an individual loan will emerge in sequence—along with closing instructions and, of course, an envelope addressed to the particular title company, escrow agent, or attorney who happens to have been designated as closing officer. The printer will generate each form and, at the same time, fill it in—untouched by human hands.

BRAVE NEW WORLD—BUT WHAT DO THE ATTORNEYS DO? Lawyers in traditional practices, with traditional legal educations, may feel queasy about the way that documents are produced at Cortelli and Barnes. After all, the classical legal education emphasizes the uniqueness of each transaction.

But Cortelli and Barnes is able to generate all the necessary numbers, select the right forms, and complete them appropriately, often with several dozen legal documents per closing, for thousands of residential loans per month. As of the time of this writing, the firm charges less than $ 200 per transaction, on the average. Simply put, the service provided by Cortelli and Barnes helps people realize the American dream of home ownership.

If every residential loan were viewed as a unique transaction in which every provision had to be reinvented, documentation for today's residential loans would be extraordinarily expensive. The approach of classical legal education, emphasizing original drafting of each paragraph, would make the cost prohibitive. Furthermore, if documents were drafted individually, from scratch, no one could be sure what they meant, or that they were complete, or that they complied with applicable law.

The real test of Cortelli and Barnes' practice is whether the firm can tailor the product to the needs of residential home buyers. The answer is subject to debate, but it seems to be "yes." When consumer demand requires a particular approach, the firm's lender clients are spurred by the marketplace to provide it. And Cortelli and Barnes is quick to supply the necessary paperwork—by generating a hand-fed form, if that is what is appropriate. If a document will be prepared thousands of times, the electronic equipment is set up to produce it. But if it is to be prepared twenty times, a fill-in-the blank form is typed and photocopied. Efficiency is important, but so is flexibility.

And it may be reassuring to learn that Cortelli and Barnes' process is not error-free. It sometimes happens, for example, that an operator erroneously keys a figure of "1" rather than the correct figure, "2," into the system. The computer catches errors that prevent its proper function in preparing the loan documents, but if the erroneous transaction is a possible one, the computer will incorporate the error into the document it produces. To prevent such errors, each set of papers is proofread three times, by three different people.

And the attorneys?

Two are kept busy on a fairly continuous basis by the process itself—a regulatory lawyer and a real estate lawyer. The need to respond to changes in lending practices, state laws, and federal regulations requires their full attention.

In every instance, lawyers have been the primary designers of the production system. Lawyers in the State at issue, working in concert with Cortelli and Barnes, help to design each new set of forms and to update the system in response to change.

THE POINT TO THIS APPENDIX. The "systems" approach, in which a unified method of interviewing, data collection, document preparation and other steps is used to make legal representation more effective and efficient, has been of interest to skilled practitioners for many years. It begins with an analysis of the discrete tasks necessary to the performance of a prototypical legal service. It must allow for individual variations, yet it can result in better performance of even idiosyncratic services because it provides a baseline from which deviations can be taken. The systems concept is applicable to other fields of law as well: to litigation, to corporate practice, domestic relations, etc.

The widespread application of computers to legal tasks has increased the advantages of a systems approach.

It remains necessary for lawyers to be able to analyze individual problems. In the handling of its other practice, in the corporate and litigation area, Cortelli and Barnes uses different approaches. It is just as important to recognize matters that must be handled outside the system as it is to have the system.

But in the real estate area, the lawyers at Cortelli and Barnes see their system as freeing them to think—and to practice law in the classical manner.

CHAPTER SEVEN

OWNERSHIP AND RESALE OF THE PROPERTY

INTRODUCTORY NOTE

Ownership of the property in fee simple did not permit the Pyneses to use it in whatever manner they wished, nor did it leave them free of obligations. The "Declaration of Covenants, Conditions and Restrictions," referred to in the chapter on Title Insurance, set certain limits on their use and required them to pay periodic fees. The Declaration also gave authority to a "homeowners association" to perform maintenance and quasi-regulatory functions, which both benefited the Pyneses and limited them. In addition, they were subject to law of the State of West York and City of London regulating the use of land. This chapter deals with those issues.

Additionally, this chapter tells the story of the resale of the property by the Pyneses. It was sold to a purchaser who "assumed the mortgage," or in other words who undertook the obligation to pay the remaining purchase money indebtedness. This transaction required documentation similar in many respects to that in the purchase by the Pyneses, but there were important differences.

A. THE RESTRICTIVE COVENANTS

NOTE ON DECLARATION OF COVENANTS

The instrument that follows is, in a sense, "out of sequence:" it was created before the Pyneses bought the property.

However, it became relevant to the Pyneses as purchasers of the property once they had acquired ownership, because it both limited and protected their exercise of ownership rights, and that is why it appears at this point in the book.

You will recall from Chapter Five that Richard Merhite, the developer of the Leebrook Town House Subdivision, conveyed the platted land to Dade Corporation, an entity set up for the purpose of developing and marketing the subdivision. As part of the normal course of developing a subdivision of townhouses, Dade made and recorded the Declaration that follows.

DECLARATION OF COVENANTS ("DEED RESTRICTIONS")

DECLARATION
OF
COVENANTS, CONDITIONS AND RESTRICTIONS

THIS DECLARATION, made on the date hereinafter set forth by DADE CORPORATION, a Texas corporation, hereinafter referred to as "Declarant",

WITNESSETH:

WHEREAS, Declarant is the owner of certain property in the County of Harris, State of Texas, which is more particularly described as:
Lots Forty-Four (44) through Sixty-Seven (67) and Lots One Hundred Fourteen (114) through One Hundred Thirty-Six (136), in Block Two (2) of LEEBROOK TOWN HOUSE SUBDIVISION, a subdivision in Manero County, West York, according to the map or plat thereof recorded in Volume 203, Page 87 of the Map Records of Harris County, Texas;

AND WHEREAS, Declarant will convey the said properties, subject to certain protective covenants, conditions, restrictions, reservations, liens and charges as hereinafter set forth;

NOW, THEREFORE, Declarant hereby declares that all of the properties described above shall be held, sold and conveyed subject to the following easements, restrictions, covenants and conditions, all of which are for the purpose of enhancing and protecting the value, desirability, and attractiveness of the real property. These easements, covenants, restrictions and conditions shall run with the real property and shall be binding on all parties having or acquiring any right, title or interest in the described properties or any part thereof, and shall inure to the benefit of each owner thereof.

[At this point, the instrument contains the following provisions:

[Article I contains definitions of basic terms (e.g., "common area," "member," "association" (meaning Leebrook Townhouse Association, which is created by the instrument), etc.

[Article II allows the Declarant, i.e. Dade Corporation, to add other real property to the subdivision, increasing its size, at certain times and under certain conditions.

[Article III makes any person who is an owner of a fee interest in any lot in the subdivision a member of the association (the Leebrook Townhouse Association).

[Article IV provides for voting rights in the association. These rights are structured to give each townhouse lot one vote (class A membership). However, during an interim period, the declarant corporation holds what is denominated class B membership; this membership gives it four votes for each unsold lot it holds. The class B membership is to cease to exist when class A votes equal class B votes (or in 1990, whichever is earlier). The effect of this provision, of course, is to give the developer control over the association until four-fifths of the lots are sold.

[Article V gives each association member a right of use of the Common Area, subject to certain conditions.

[The instrument then continues with the following Article VI:]

ARTICLE VI
COVENANT FOR MAINTENANCE ASSESSMENTS

Section 1. Creation of the Lien and Personal Obligation of Assessments. The Declarant, for each Lot owned within the Properties, hereby covenants, and each Owner of any Lot by acceptance of a deed therefor, whether or not it shall be so expressed in any such deed or other conveyance, is deemed to covenant and agreed to pay to the Association: (1) annual assessment or charges, and (2) special assessments for capital improvements and subdivision maintenance services, including but not limited to gas or electric current for street lamps and garbage collection, such assessments to be fixed, established, and collected from time to time as hereinafter provided. The annual and special assessments, together with such interest thereon and costs of collection thereof, as hereinafter provided, shall be a charge on the land and shall be a continuing lien upon the Property against which each such assessment is made. Each such assessment, together with such interest, costs, and reasonable attorney's fees shall also be the personal obligation of the person who was the Owner of such property at the time when the assessment fell due * * *. The personal obligation shall not pass to his successors in title unless expressly assumed by them.

[The instrument continues with provisions governing the use of these maintenance assessments, special assessments for capital improvements voted by a 2/3 margin, exemption of common areas, etc. from the assessments, insurance assessments, mortgage holders' payment in the event of default by the member, and like provisions. The assessment is limited to $144 per lot through 2001. After that date, the ceiling may be increased by a vote of 2/3 of the property members. The assessment is required to be uniform across all lots.

[The instrument then continues with the following Article VII:]

ARTICLE VII
ARCHITECTURAL CONTROL

No building shall be erected, placed or altered on any of said Lots until the building plans, specifications and plot plan showing the location of such building have been approved in writing as to conformity and harmony of external design with existing structures in the subdivision, and as to location of them with respect to topography and finished ground elevation by a committee composed of John Sheehan, Philip McQuarles and Rachel E. Linebarger, or a representative designated by a majority of the members of said committee.* * * In the event said committee, or its designated representative, fails to approve or disapprove such design and location within thirty (30) days after said plans and specifications have been submitted to it, or in any event, if no suit to enjoin the erection of such building or the making of such alterations has been commenced prior to the completion thereof, such approval will not be required and this covenant will be deemed to have been fully complied with.* * *

[The instrument contains certain other provisions governing the architectural committee; for example, it provides that in 2002 and thereafter, the committee shall be composed of three association members elected by all members.

[The instrument contains, then, an Article VIII which provides a detailed list of "Do's" and "Dont's" for individual homeowners. These are the kind of restrictions one would expect for the enhancement of a residential area, including prohibitions on the conduct of businesses; limits on trash, exterior remodeling, storage of building materials, etc.; requirements for upkeep of vegetation and so forth. Some representative restrictions are the following:]

Section 9. No cattle, horses, mules, sheep, rabbits, hogs, poultry, or other animals or fowl other than ordinary household pets may be kept on any Lot; and no person shall keep either cats, dogs, birds, or other household pets in such quantity as to be reasonably considered to annoy the neighbors, it being the sense of these restrictions that reasonable keeping of pets shall be permitted, but that the increase thereof must be removed from the premises with reasonable dispatch, and none may be kept, bred, or maintained for commercial purposes.

Section 10. No privy, cesspool, tank, or disposal plant shall be erected or maintained on any Lot.

Section 11. No operation of any kind shall be conducted on any Lot to explore for, produce, store, treat, or transport oil, gas or other minerals.

[The provision ends with restrictions upon temporary homes, trailers, fences, exterior antennas and the like.

[Thereafter, the instrument contains the following articles:

[Article IX, providing for maintenance of records about mortgages, notices to mortgagees of defaults in connection with the instrument, and other provisions designed to ease financing.

[Article X, governing party walls between units.]

ARTICLE XI
EXTERIOR MAINTENANCE

In addition to maintenance upon the Common Area, the Association shall provide exterior maintenance upon each Lot which is subject to assessment hereunder, as follows: paint, repair, replace and care for roofs, gutters, down-spouts, exterior building surfaces, trees, shrubs, grass, walks, and other exterior improvements. Such exterior maintenance shall not include glass surfaces, doors and door fixtures, patios, and associated hardware nor shall it include shrubbery, trees or grass contained within patio fences or hardware used in connection with these items.

[Article XII creates certain easements (including utility easements, easements for entry to perform maintenance duties, etc.

[Article XIII governs enforcement of restrictions and term of the instrument. It is effective through the year 2035 unless extended for 10-year terms by the vote of a majority of association members.

[The instrument is executed and acknowledged by both the landowner (which is the Declarant, Dade Corp.) and the holder of the deed of trust (Park Bank).]

B. ZONING AND OTHER LAND USE RESTRICTIONS

NOTE

Although detailed treatment of land use regulation is beyond the scope of this book, it may be interesting to place this property in its regulatory context in a general way.

The Leebrook Town House Subdivision was subject to a zoning ordinance of the City of London, zoning it as "Class B-2" (permitting high density single-family dwellings). The zoning ordinance was in some respects a more general version of the restrictive covenants (for example, it prohibited commercial activities on premises in the area).

The City of London has no ordinances regulating growth as a general proposition. In recent years, agencies of the city and county that approve plats, grant sewer permits, and perform other nominally more ministerial functions have been forced to consider factors related to the "desirable" rate of growth of the City of London. This phenomenon has led to both legal and political challenges to such use of authority.

C. ESTABLISHMENT OF THE HOMEOWNERS ASSOCIATION

ARTICLES OF INCORPORATION OF
LEEBROOK TOWNHOUSE ASSOCIATION, INC.

In compliance with the requirements of the State of West York, the undersigned, all of whom are citizens of the State of West York and all of whom are over the age of 18 years, have this day voluntarily associated themselves together for the purpose of forming a corporation not for profit and do hereby certify:

ARTICLE I
NAME

The name of the corporation is LEEBROOK TOWNHOUSE ASSOCIATION, INC., hereinafter called the "Association".

ARTICLE II
NON-PROFIT

The corporation is a non-profit corporation.

ARTICLE III
DURATION

The period of duration is perpetual.

ARTICLE IV
REGISTERED AGENT

The initial registered office of the Association is located at 806 Baugh Drive, London, W.Y., and the initial registered agent at such address is Edwin Fowler.

* * *

[The articles of incorporation also contain the following:

[Article V, the "purpose clause," which establishes the purposes and powers of the corporation (including "maintenance, preservation and architectural control" of the property);

[Article VI, making all fee owners members;

[Article VII, setting out the voting rights specified in the Declarations;

[Article VIII, creating a 3-member board of directors and naming the first directors (3 individuals connected with the developer);

[Article IX, setting a limit on indebtedness;

[Article X, allowing mortgaging of the common area only by a vote of 2/3 of the membership;

[Article XI, giving the right to dedicate parts of the common area for public use (i.e., roads) only by a 2/3 vote;

[Article XII, relating to dissolution;

[Article XIII, requiring a 75 per cent vote for amendments; and

[Article XVI, setting forth the names and addresses of the three statutorily required incorporators.
[The instrument is signed and acknowledged by the incorporators.]

BY-LAWS OF THE ASSOCIATION

BY-LAWS OF LEEBROOK TOWNHOUSE ASSOCIATION, INC.

ARTICLE I
NAME AND LOCATION

The name of the corporation is LEEBROOK TOWNHOUSE ASSOCIATION, INC., hereinafter referred to as the "Association". The principal office of the corporation shall be located at *2530 Winston, Suite 300*, London, West York, but meetings of members and directors may be held at such places within the State of West York, County of Manero, as may be designated by the Board of Directors.

ARTICLE II
DEFINITIONS

Section 1.   "Association" shall mean and refer to LEEBROOK Townhouse Association, Inc., its successors and assigns.

* * *

[The by-laws govern the way the association runs its affairs, in a more specific manner than the articles of incorporation. For example, the by-laws provide for director's meetings, specify the manner of election of directors, set out the powers of the board of directors, and create a term of office for directors. They also require the appointment of an Architectural Control Committee, and specify that the board shall appoint other appropriate committees (such as recreation, maintenance, publicity and audit committees). They require annual meetings of members (shareholders' meetings, in effect). They provide for the election and powers and duties of a president, vice-president, secretary and treasurer. They incorporate a large portion of the requirements of the declaration of covenants and restrictions (such as the provisions regarding assessments). They also contain formal provisions pertaining to the keeping and inspection of books and records of the corporation, pertaining to the corporate seal, and pertaining to amendments by majority vote. The by-laws are signed by the members of the board of directors.

[The following provision is an example:]

ARTICLE V
BOARD OF DIRECTORS: SELECTION: TERM OF OFFICE

Section 1.   Number.   The affairs of this Association shall be managed by a Board of three (3) directors, who need not be Members of the Association.

Section 2.   Election.   At the first annual meeting the Members shall elect one director for a term of one year, one director for a term of two years and one director for a term of three years; and at each annual meeting thereafter the members shall elect one director for a term of three years.

Section 3.   Removal.   Any director may be removed from the Board, with or without cause, by a majority vote of the Members of the Association.   In the event of death, resignation or removal of a director, his successor shall be selected by the remaining members of the Board and shall serve for the unexpired term of his predecessor.

Section 4.   Compensation.   No director shall receive compensation for any service he may render to the Association.   However, any director may be reimbursed for his actual expenses incurred in the performance of his duties.

Section 5.   Action Taken Without a Meeting.   The directors shall have the right to take any action in the absence of a meeting which they could take at a meeting by obtaining the written approval of all the directors.   Any action so approved shall have the same effect as though taken at a meeting of the directors.

* * *

D. FUNCTIONS OF THE HOMEOWNERS ASSOCIATION (ILLUSTRATIVE DOCUMENTS)

MINUTES OF A HOMEOWNERS ASSOCIATION MEETING

MINUTES OF ANNUAL MEETING OF HOMEOWNERS (2014)

CALL TO ORDER & QUORUM. The annual meeting of the members of Leebrook Townhouse Association was called to order at 7:00 p.m. on Monday, August 6, 2014, at Leebrook Community Center, 6550 Winger Road, London, W.Y., with Tanya McNeese, President, presiding. A quorum was certified, being sixteen (16) people. All members of the board were present.

MINUTES: TREASURER'S REPORT. Minutes of the last annual meeting were presented and approved as presented. Cary Dole gave the Treasurer's report, which was received and approved. By unanimous consent, it was agreed that the Treasurer's report would be incorporated into these minutes.

DIRECTORS, OFFICERS & COMMITTEES. A new director, Leaver Grimes, was elected to serve a three-year term. The association's officers were re-elected and remain as Tanya McNeese, President; Leaver Grimes, Vice-president; Cary Dole, Treasurer; and Seth Denckla, Secretary. New Committees were elected, as follows: Sharon Grimes, Lawn Maintenance; Bill Herskowitz, Architectural Control.

MONTHLY MAINTENANCE ASSESSMENT. The Board recommended an increase in the maintenance fee from $ 65.00 per month to $ 75.00 per month. The motion was made by Linda Perry and seconded by Cary Dole. Open discussion about repainting, roofing, and various maintenance work followed. The past year was one of various natural and man-made disasters, and Hurricane Alicia resulted in exterior damage as well as collections of trash which your Board was required to expend enormous sums to remove. Discussion centered upon whether a special capital assessment or an increase in the monthly assessment was appropriate. The motion carried, and the $ 75.00 maintenance fee is effective September 1, 2014.

DELINQUENCIES IN ASSESSMENTS. There is still a great deal of concern by your Board and by most townhouse owners about the delinquencies in the payment of maintenance fees by some owners. The newly constituted Board is determined to use any and all means available, including employment of counsel and initiation of foreclosure proceedings, to bring all accounts to a current status. President McNeese noted that attorney's fees of the association become payable by the delinquent member.

ARCHITECTURAL CONTROL. Bill Herskowitz reminded all present that any alteration of the structure or exterior of your premises requires the approval of the Architectural Control Committee. This requirement applies to fences. If a homeowner creates a structure such as a fence without the approval of the Committee, it will be necessary for the structure to be removed. Don't let this happen to you.

LAWN MAINTENANCE. * * *

ATTACHMENTS. Projected maintenance requirements, financial statements, and other parts of the Treasurer's report are attached.

Seth G. Denckla
Seth Denckla, Secretary

LONG-TERM MAINTENANCE PROJECTIONS

LEEBROOK TOWNHOUSES
Projection of Major Items of Recurring Maintenance Expense

Item No.	Description	Estimated Cost--Date		Frequency Years
1.	Dwelling Unit Roofing	60,000	2020	15
2.	Carport Roofing	28,000	2020	15
3.	Exterior Building Paint	18,000	2016	3
4.	Carport Paint	2,000	2016	3
5.	Patio Fencing Posts/Boards	12,500	2025	20/15
6.	Patio Fencing Boards	7,500	2020	15

BALANCE SHEET

Leebrook Townhouse Association, Inc.
Statement of Assets, Liabilities and Owners' Equity
July 31, 2014 and July 31, 2013

	2014	2013
Assets		
Current Assets		
Cash in Bank - Checking Account	$20,970.93	$10,338.13
Cash in Bank - Savings Account	9,432.86	7,808.39
Certificate of Deposit	10,000.00	10,000.00
Dreyfus Tax Exempt Bond Fund (Market - 1983, $12,626.62; 1982, $11,315.88)	13,183.01	12,107.31
Accounts Receivable - Owners	3,640.00	2,610.00
Accrued Interest	43.84	270.90
Prepaid Insurance	396.89	775.65
Total Assets	$57,667.53	$43,910.38
Liabilities and Owners' Equity		
Current Liabilities		
Monthly Maintenance - Paid in Advance	$ 250.00	$ 0.00
Federal Income Tax Payable	389.22	434.15
Accounts Payable	0.00	1,155.00
Total Current Liabilities	639.22	1,589.15
Owners' Equity		
Maintenance Reserve	2,050.00	2,050.00
Excess Assessments, Beginning of Year	40,271.23	28,472.02
Excess Assessments, For Year	14,707.08	11,799.21
Total Owners' Equity	57,028.31	42,321.23
Total Liabilities and Owners' Equity	$57,667.53	$43,910.38

The accountant's letter and accompanying notes are
an integral part of this statement.

E. NOTES AND QUESTIONS ON LAND USE RESTRICTIONS AND HOMEOWNERS ASSOCIATION

1. THE DEED RESTRICTIONS. The restrictions are a kind of "private zoning," if the metaphor is apt. In many cities, in fact, such privately imposed restrictions are more important than zoning, and there are a few major cities that have no (or very little) zoning. The only prohibition upon the opening of a gas station in one's neighbor's lot in such a city is the restrictions.

2. FORCE OF THE RESTRICTIONS. What happens (or what should happen) if Edgar Pynes hangs a sign upon his door saying, "Offices of Edgar Pynes," and commences to conduct a chemical engineering consulting practice at that location? The restrictions prohibit the conduct of any "business." Further, the restrictions contain a provision authorizing any other homeowner to enforce the covenants by injunction or suit for damages (and to recover reasonable attorney's fees). "Violations" are often ambiguous, however (is Pynes in violation if he sets aside a study in which he maintains engineering drawing equipment and often sees potential clients in his living room?)

3. LAPSE OF THE RESTRICTIONS. Restrictions are often written so that they must be renewed after a period of time (periods as short as five years or as long as 99 are common). Typically, the question of renewal is controlled by the vote of a majority. It makes a great difference whether the restrictions are written so that they renew unless there is a vote to the contrary or whether they are written so that they lapse in the absence of a vote (theoretically, there would be only one vote difference between these two arrangements; can you see why the difference is greater as a practical matter?) In addition, restrictions may be considered unenforceable in the event of "changed conditions." This term of art means such an alteration of the subdivision or its environs that enforcement is no longer reasonable or equitable. Lengthy toleration of multiple deviations from the restrictions can give rise to "changed conditions." If you were an attorney representing a homeowner s association, what advice would you therefore give about action against violators?

4. RESTRICTIVE COVENANTS AS VERSUS ZONING OR OTHER PUBLIC LAND USE LAW. In theory, much of what can be accomplished by restrictions can be accomplished by zoning. But zoning must be done according to a relatively uniform jurisdiction-wide system, creates difficult questions of fairness and legality, and involves a process that can be cumbersome and even corrupt. Even if there are zoning prohibitions that currently protect a given interest, private covenants may be useful. They provide a means of tailoring the prohibitions to a given subdivision. Of course, zoning may protect interests that cross subdivision lines (what happens if an offending industrial plant is established just opposite this small subdivision and is not subject to the privately adopted restrictions at issue here?)

5. THE HOMEOWNERS ASSOCIATION. The association was organized as a non-profit corporation, and it was possible to structure it so that assessments were tax exempt (you may have noted that the financial statements contain a reserve for taxes, but that is for income from interest, dividends and the like). The articles of incorporation are in standard form for a non-profit corporation. Obviously, to be a real estate lawyer, one must also be a corporate lawyer and a tax lawyer.

6. POWERS AND DUTIES OF THE HOMEOWNERS ASSOCIATION. The powers and duties of the association are defined by the restrictive covenants and by the articles and by-laws. However, there may be ambiguities. For example, the covenants, here, provide that the association "shall provide exterior maintenance upon each Lot. . . . Such exterior maintenance shall not include glass surfaces, doors and door fixtures. . . ." Question: may the Board of Directors cause broken windows to be repaired, using capital improvement assessments? May it refuse to repair a structure added to the exterior by an individual homeowner? In the exercise of its authority to make capital improvements to the common areas, may it install an expensive handball court which is desired by 70 percent of the membership but vehemently opposed by others?

7. THE "MAINTENANCE FEE." Notice the increase in monthly assessments for each lot (at $75.00 per month, the total is $900 per year). What protection do dissenting homeowners have against increases they consider unreasonable? (Other than their own votes, persuasion of other votes, and restric-

tions on types of expenditures in the covenants, is there any protection? Are such protections adequate? Would greater protection be desirable?)

8. **OFFICERS AND DIRECTORS OF THE ASSOCIATION.** Officers and directors have quasi-fiduciary responsibilities as in any corporation. What will be your response if, upon opening a busy law practice, the homeowners or condominium association where you live calls upon you to serve as an officer?

F. "TRANSFER" OF THE PROPERTY AS BETWEEN THE TWO OWNERS

DECLARATION OF BENEFICIAL OWNERSHIP

The undersigned, Andrew B. Pynes, does by these presents declare that he holds such interest as he may hold in that certain real property at 7947 Brainerd Lane, London, West York, in Trust only, as trustee for Edgar E. Pynes. Edgar E. Pynes hereby agrees to indemnify and hold harmless Andrew B. Pynes from any and all damages, claims, indebtednesses and payments in connection with such property. This Declaration is Executed on September 1, 2014, but it is declaratory of a trust relationship that existed as of the instant of the acquisition of the property on June 30, 2014.
Executed by:

Andrew B. Pynes
Edgar E. Pynes

NOTE ON TRANSFER OF EQUITABLE INTEREST

This document is designed to establish that Edgar Pynes "really owns" the property. The probability is that Andrew and Edgar have agreed among themselves that Edgar will pay all indebtedness and obtain the benefits and burdens of the property; Andrew is in the picture only because the S&L insisted that he be on the note (remember Chapter 3).

A number of questions should arise in your mind about this instrument. First, it may not satisfy the Statute of Frauds (if the courts of the State interpret the Statute to require a description of the property equivalent in specificity to a metes and bounds or plat description, as some decisions do, it is inadequate for that reason alone). Secondly, it might be interpreted as enabling the Lender to accelerate pursuant to the due-on-sale clause. (Is this a "transfer" without Lender's consent of an "interest" in the property?) Third, the instrument is not acknowledged and therefore not recordable, and, if unrecorded, it would not prevent Andrew Pynes' legal interest from being alienated by any one of a variety of means. Fourth, should the document also provide that Andrew holds title in trust not only for Edgar, but also for himself, as security for Edgar's promise to hold Andrew harmless from payments on the property?

The use of a formal Declaration of Beneficial Ownership is common in many States to accomplish written recognition that property is beneficially owned by a person other than the person who holds legal title. (A handwritten declaration was in fact executed in the transaction that this book is based upon, in a form similar to but slightly different from this document.) Since the transaction is "all in the family," it might be thought that informality does no harm. However, the very purpose of the document is probably to protect against the possibility that the elder Pynes might die, become disabled or otherwise be unable to ensure protection of Edgar's full ownership, and in that event, formalities might become important.

G. RESALE: A NEW PURCHASER "ASSUMES THE MORTGAGE"

NOTE ON RESALE OF THE PROPERTY

Effective January 1985, West York Chemical Company transferred Edgar Pynes to its Eastern Seaboard Facility, located in another State.

Edgar put the townhouse on the market again. Within a short time, it had been purchased. The buyers were Gunther and Emily Piotrowski.

Many of the steps in the resale of the property were similar to those in the original transaction, by which Edgar purchased from Park Bank. Edgar employed a broker, who procured the Piotrowski's signatures on a purchase and sale contract. The contract provided for a closing, at which a note, deed and security agreement were executed. A policy of title insurance was obtained after a process similar to that in preceding chapters.

In the materials that follow, repetition is minimized. Only the clauses that would be expected to differ markedly from those in the previous transaction are emphasized here.

ASSUMPTION SALE CONTRACT

ASSUMPTION OF LOAN — RESIDENTIAL EARNEST MONEY CONTRACT

1. PARTIES: _Edgar and Andrew Pynes_____ (Seller) agrees to sell and convey to _Gunther and Emily Piotrowski_____ (Buyer) and Buyer agrees to buy from Seller the following property situated in _Mansero County, West York,_ known as _7947 Brainerd Lane, London, West York_ (Address).
2. PROPERTY: Lot _65_____, Block _2_____, _Cedarbrook Town House_ _Subdivision_ Addition, City of _London, Mansero County, West York_ or as described on attached exhibit, together with the following fixtures, if any: curtain rods, drapery rods, venetian blinds, window shades, screens and shutters, awnings, wall-to-wall carpeting, mirrors fixed in place, attic fans, permanently installed heating and air conditioning units and equipment, lighting and plumbing fixtures, TV antennas, mail boxes, water softeners, shrubbery and all other property owned by Seller and attached to the above described real property. All property sold by this contract is called "Property".

---

3. CONTRACT SALES PRICE:
   A. The ☒ Exact ☐ Approximate   Cash down payment payable at closing . . . . $ _220,500.00_

   B. Buyer's assumption of the unpaid balance of a promissory note (the Note) payable in present monthly installments of $ _____, including principal and interest and any reserve deposits, with Buyer's first
   installment payable to _Huntington Savings Association_
   on _January 1_ , _2015_, the assumed principal balance of which at closing
   (allowing for an agreed $250 variance) will be . . . . $ _600,000.00_

   C. Any balance of Sales Price to be evidenced by a second lien note payable to [check (1) or (2) below]:
   ☒ (1) Seller, bearing interest at the rate of _____0_____ % per annum, in
       ☐ lump sum on or before _____ _plus interest_
       ☒ principal and interest installments of $ _1600.00_ / , or more per _six months_
       with first installment payable on _July 1, 2015_

   ☐ (2) Third Party in principal and interest installments not in excess of $ _____ per month
   and in the ☐ Exact ☐ Approximate (check "Approximate" only if A above and D below are "Exact")
   amount of . . . . $ _5,000.00_ *
   *_plus interest_

   D. The ☒ Exact ☐ Approximate total Sales Price of (Sum of A, B and C above) . . . . $ _825,500.00_ *

4. FINANCING CONDITIONS: If a Noteholder on assumption (i) requires Buyer to pay an assumption fee in excess of $ _4,000.00_
   and Seller declines to pay such excess (ii) raises the existing interest rate above _4.25_ % or (iii) requires approval of Buyer or can accelerate the Note and Buyer does not receive from the Noteholder written approval and acceleration waiver prior to the Closing Date, Buyer
   may terminate this contract and the Earnest Money shall be refunded. Buyer shall apply for the approval and waiver under (iii) above within 7
   days from the effective date hereof and shall make every reasonable effort to obtain the same.

NOTE ON MECHANICS OF THE ASSUMPTION SALE

The relatively short time that Edgar Pynes had held the property made an "assumption sale" appropriate.

If Pynes had owned the townhouse for a period of many years, and if the market value therefore greatly exceeded the loan balance, new financing would likely be needed. The new financing would have involved the following principal steps: buyers would (1) obtain a loan from a lender in the amount of the purchase price less their down payment, (2) give the new lender a mortgage or deed of trust, and (3) use part of the loan proceeds to pay Pyne's remaining indebtedness on the old note. But since the loan balance was close to its original amount and there had not been a long period of appreciation, the most efficient approach was for the Piotrowskis to assume the obligation to pay the indebtedness to Huntington Savings and to pay a sum to Pynes representing the market value of his equity in the property.

The contract, above, sets out the terms of this particular assumption sale. The total consideration of $825,500 is to consist of the assumption of the loan, plus payment of $225,500 to Edgar Pynes, part of which is to be paid over time. Pynes will be secured by a second lien—or, in the parlance of the trade, will "take a second." This arrangement is sometimes called "owner financing."

Certain excerpts from the closing documents follow.

DEED (ADAPTED FOR ASSUMPTION SALE WITH OWNER FINANCING)

A S S U M P T I O N
WARRANTY DEED WITH VENDOR'S LIEN

THE STATE OF WEST YORK

COUNTY OF MANERO
          } KNOW ALL PERSONS BY THESE PRESENTS:

That we, EDGAR E. PYNES and ANDREW B. PYNES, herein called Grantors, of the County of   Manero   and State of   West York   for and in

consideration of the sum of   TEN and no/100- -

- ($10.00)- - DOLLARS

and other valuable consideration to the undersigned paid by the grantee s herein named, the receipt of which

is hereby acknowledged, and the further consideration of the express assumption of and the express agreement to pay by the Grantees herein, prior to delinquency, and as the same matures, the unpaid principal balance, $ 600,000 , with interest accrued from January 1, 2015, due and owing on that certain note dated June 30, 2014, executed by Edgar E. Pynes and Andrew B. Pynes, made payable to the order of Huntington Savings Association, in monthly installments, including interest, secured by Deed of Trust dated June 30, 2014 to Albert R. Ballard, Trustee, filed under Manero County Clerk's File No. G738216, and recorded under Film Code No. 7281-39-7423, Real Property Records of Manero County, West York,

the payment of which note is secured by the vendor's lien herein retained, and is additionally secured by a deed

of trust of even date herewith to   KARL V. WALKER,   Trustee,

have GRANTED, SOLD AND CONVEYED, and by these presents do GRANT, SELL AND CONVEY unto GUNTHER A. PIOTROWSKI and EMILY R. PIOTROWSKI, Husband and Wife,

of the County of   Manero   and State of West York, all of the following described real

property in Manero County, W.Y.,   to-wit:

[The property description, habendum, warranty, reservation of vendor's lien, exceptions to title, execution, and acknowledgements follow here.]

SECURITY INSTRUMENT ASSURING PAYMENTS TO ORIGINAL LENDER

[Although the instrument that follows is in the form of a deed of trust, the basic idea is universal and can equally well be embodied in a straight mortgage. Remember the purpose of this instrument: the sellers (the Pynses) remain liable to the original lender (Huntington Savings) and are dependent on the buyers (the Piotrowskis) to discharge that liability since they have assumed the obligation, and this document enables the Pyneses to foreclose if they fail to make payments appropriately.]

MORTGAGE/DEED OF TRUST
TO SECURE ASSUMPTION

THE STATE WEST YORK   }
COUNTY OF MANERO   } KNOW ALL PERSONS BY THESE PRESENTS:

That GUNTHER A. PIOTROWSKI and EMILY R. PIOTROWSKI, husband and wife, of Manero County, W.Y., hereinafter called Grantors (whether one or more) for the purpose of securing the indebtedness hereinafter described, and in consideration of the sum of TEN DOLLARS ($10.00) to us in hand paid by the Trustee hereinafter named, the receipt of which is hereby acknowledged, and for the further consideration of the uses, purposes and trusts hereinafter set forth, have granted, sold and conveyed, and by these presents do grant, sell and convey unto Karl V. Walker, Trustee, of Manero County, W.Y., and his substitutes or successors, all of the following described property situated in Manero County, West York, to wit:

[The property description and habendum follow at this point, but are omitted in this reproduction.]

This conveyance, however, is made in TRUST for the following purposes:
WHEREAS, EDGAR E. PYNES and ANDREW B. PYNES,

hereinafter called Beneficiary, by deed of even date herewith conveyed the herein described property to Grantors named herein, who, as part of the consideration therefor assumed and promised to pay, according to the terms thereof, all principal and interest remaining unpaid upon that one certain promissory note in the original principal sum of $ 600,000
June 30, 2014   executed by Edgar E. Pynes and
Andrew B. Pynes,
and payable to order of Huntington Savings Association,

* * *

[The instrument here recites the circumstances, including the assumption of the obligation by the Piotrowskis ("Grantors")].

Grantors agree that in the event of default in the payment of any installment, principal or interest, of the note so assumed by Grantors, or in the event of default in the payment of said note when due or declared due, or of a breach of any of the obligations or covenants contained in the Deed of Trust securing said note so assumed, Beneficiary may, at his option, advance and pay such sum or sums as may be required to cure any such default, and that any and all such sums so advanced and paid by Beneficiary to cure such default shall be paid by Grantors to Beneficiary at their respective then residences   in the City of their respective then residences,   within five (5) days after the date of such payment, without notice or demand, which are expressly waived.

Grantors covenant to pay promptly to Beneficiary, without notice or demand, within the time and as provided in the foregoing paragraph, any and all sums that may, under the provisions of the foregoing paragraph, be due Beneficiary.

* * *

[The instrument here creates a power of private sale on behalf of the Pyneses in the event of default upon the assumption.

[Remaining provisions of the instrument concluding with the Piotrowskis' execution and acknowledgements are omitted.]

NOTE COVERING "OWNER FINANCING"
REAL ESTATE LIEN NOTE
(SUBORDINATE)

$5,000.00   January 1, 2015

For value received, I, We, or either of us, as principals, promise to pay to the order of ....
.... EDGAR E. PYNES ....

in the City of London, Manero County, West York,   the sum of
FIVE THOUSAND and no/100 --
--Dollars ($5,000.00----) in legal and lawful
money of the United States of America, with interest thereon from date hereof until maturity at the rate of
---- Ten ------- per cent (_10_%) per annum; the interest payable at six-month intervals;
matured unpaid principal and interest shall bear interest at the rate of ten per cent (10%) per annum from date of maturity until paid.

This note is due and payable as follows, to-wit:

In installments of $1,000.00 each, plus interest then accrued, the first such installment to be due and payable on or before

July 1, 2014, and a like installment of principal plus interest then accrued to be due and payable on or before each succeeding first day of January and first day of July until the whole of this note, both principal and interest, shall be fully and finally paid.

* * *

[The remaining portions of this instrument provide for acceleration, reservation of a vendor's lien, and other remedies, and are omitted in this reproduction.]

SECURITY INSTRUMENT SECURING "OWNER FINANCING"

[In addition to the securing of the assumption, which protects the seller with respect to his obligations to the original lender, the seller would normally require a Mortgage or Deed of Trust to secure the note to. himself, the seller. If in Deed of Trust form, the instrument would grant to a trustee, with power of private sale, providing substantially as follows:]

SUBORDINATE ("SECOND") MORTGAGE/DEED OF TRUST

* * *

This conveyance, however, is made in TRUST to secure payment of one certain promissory note of even

date herewith in the principal sum of FIVE THOUSAND and no/100 -----------------

--- Dollars ($ 5,000.00---)

executed by Grantors, payable to the order of EDGAR E. PYNES

in the City of London, Manero County, West York,

In installments of $ 1,000.00 each, plus interest then accrued, the first such installment to be due and payable on

* * *

[The remaining provisions of the security instrument are omitted in this reproduction.]

ESTOPPEL AND INFORMATION LETTER

West York Title Insurance Co.
London, West York 77002
Re: GF#9784--Edgar E. Pynes and Andrew B. Pynes

Dear Sir or Madam:

In accordance with your request, the following information is provided for your disposal by Huntington Savings Association:

Date of Mortgage	6/30/2014	Principal & Interest	$ 2125
Original Amount	$ 600,000	Principal Balance	$ 600,000
Term & Rate	adjustable 4.25	Escrow Balance	$ 5875
Total Payment	2125 + escrow	Past Due	none
TRANSFER FEE	$ 2500	Payment Due Date	1st, montly

We must have (1) a certified copy of the deed upon delivery; (2) an assignment of the escrow fund and hazard insurance policy; (3) a transfer fee in the amount set forth above; and (4) any past due payments or late charges, if any, set forth above, before we will be in a position to complete this transfer. * * *

H. NOTES AND QUESTIONS ON THE ASSUMPTION SALE

1. SORTING OUT THE INSTRUMENTS. Students are sometimes confused by the ancillary documents in an assumption sale, particularly when there is a second mortgage. The deed itself serves the normal functions of a deed and, in addition, recites the loan assumption obligation and expressly makes it part of the transaction. The security instrument securing the assumption (which is the instrument that most often proves confusing) is executed because the original borrower-seller remains personally liable on the original note and, therefore, wishes to be protected against the new buyer's failure to make payments as agreed. This document, in essence, allows the seller to make payments on the loan if buyer does not, and to foreclose accordingly. Finally, the note and second security instrument set forth and secure the buyer's obligation to pay the "owner financed" portion of the consideration.

2. THE "ASSUMPTION" DEED AS VERSUS THE "SUBJECT TO" DEED. Acceptance of the deed with "assumption" of the loan makes the buyer personally liable for the payment of the loan balance (as is the original borrower-seller). By way of contrast, a "subject to" deed does not personally obligate the new buyer on the loan. In other words, with a subject-to deed, the new buyer may lose his property through foreclosure if the note is not paid according to its terms, but the lender cannot obtain a personal judgment against him. This result is accomplished by insertion of language to the effect that the conveyance is "subject to the unpaid principal balance of [specified amount] due and owing on that certain note [describing it], secured by [describing the mortgage or deed of trust.]" The "subject to" deed is rarely used in residential transactions. Instead, the assumption deed is the norm, because a home purchaser would expect to be personally liable.

3. THE LENDER'S WILLINGNESS TO CONSENT TO THE ASSUMPTION. The assumption sale cannot effectively be consummated without the lender's consent, because of the due on sale clause in the security instrument (see Chapter 4). Here, the lender has previously received a loan application from the new buyers and has approved them. If the intended new owners of the property were not good credit risks, the lender would not agree to the assumption even though the original borrower remained personally liable because collection is simply more regular as a practical matter if the resident owner is a responsible borrower.

4. THE LENDER'S TERMS FOR CONSENT TO THE ASSUMPTION. The lender may also insist upon a monetary consideration for its consent (see Chapter 3). The lender's right to do so has been controversial in the past but seems to be recognized today. In this case, since the note is an adjustable one, the lender may not be strongly motivated by the desire to increase the rate of interest to the market rate, but as the documents show, it does require a transfer fee of one percent of the loan balance. Notice that the buyer benefits, because the "points" required for obtaining a new loan elsewhere would be greater than one percent. What would be likely to happen if the assumption were of an older, fixed-rate loan below the market rate? In West York, at the time of this transaction, the custom is to charge an assumption fee of one percent (as here), and also to raise the rate of interest to about one percent less than the current market. (Why less than the current market? So that the buyer is not induced to obtain a new loan from another lender. If there were no advantage to the assumption, the buyer would have no reason not to take his business elsewhere. One lenders' attorney explained the matter thus, to the authors of this book: "You want to bring him current, but you don't want to run him off.")

5. AN ALTERNATE MEANS OF ACCOMPLISHING THE ASSUMPTION: A NEW NOTE. An alternate means of accomplishing the result of an assumption is to treat the buyer as a new borrower and to draft a new note and security instrument for him to sign. The lender would naturally prefer this approach if the mortgage is adjustable and if the market rate has increased since the last adjustment; in that event, executing of a new note at the present date and rate gives the lender the benefit of a current adjustment. An "assumption" of this kind is not an assumption at all, although it is often called one because it amounts to much the same thing. In West York, as of the time of this transaction, the "new note" assumption is the common practice. The older borrower-seller typically obtains a release of his note.

6. THE "ESTOPPEL LETTER." When decisions depend upon actions or information within the control of the lender, it is customary to obtain from the lender a letter reciting the facts in question, such as the loan balance, the absence of events of default, etc.. The letter may not be enforceable as a contract or warranty, but it may create an estoppel if relied upon, and hence such a letter is frequently referred to as an "estoppel letter." Can you see why it would be useful to obtain such a letter in the course of an assumption purchase? For a variety of reasons, a lender may be reluctant to provide such a letter in some situations. What might you do if advising a purchaser in such a situation?

7. OTHER DOCUMENTS NECESSARY FOR THE ASSUMPTION. The written consent of the lender is, of course, a necessary document. In addition, certain other papers that are not necessary in the sale of a new home are necessary for an assumption; for example, the seller has built up a sum in escrow for taxes and insurance, and the custom is to assign this sum, by an instrument drawn for that purpose, to the buyer (and to take this matter into account at closing). Most of the remaining documents would not differ materially from those previously illustrated.

APPENDIX TO CHAPTER 7:
WHAT KINDS OF TAX CONSIDERATIONS AFFECT REAL ESTATE TRANSACTIONS?

Real estate lawyers must be good tax lawyers. In fact, tax considerations may "drive" a given transaction; that is to say, they may be what makes the transaction advantageous. Here are some examples, from this transaction and other transactions:

1. DEDUCTIBLE INTEREST PAYMENTS. Home mortgage interest often is deductible (and it probably would be here). This loan is an interest-only loan, so that all of the mortgage payments (not all of the escrow) are deductible. Even if it were a principal-and-interest loan, so that at the end of the term the borrower has paid the entire mortgage loan as well as interest, it probably would be structured so that most of the early payments were interest, to take advantage of the deductibility feature.

State real estate taxes on a residence may be deductible too.

If this were a commercial or business transaction—the purchase of a business location, for example—the considerations become more complex. But a purchase and sale will be structured to allow the buyer to deduct these same items if it is possible to do so.

What about the "points" (such as the origination fee) paid by the Pyneses to Huntington Savings? If they can be treated as prepaid interest, these too might be deductible. The issue requires a knowledge of tax laws.

BUT WHY DOES THIS ("DEDUCTIBILITY") MATTER? BECAUSE FOR MOST BUYERS AND SELLERS, WEALTH=GOOD BUT BIG TAXES=BAD. Often, when you are a student, taxes are not a major consideration. But when you are earning significant amounts of money, taxes are a major issue. For most of your clients, wealth is good and big taxes are bad. There are worse things than paying taxes (such as making a tax-driven bad transactions), but minimizing taxes become a major consideration. Deductions are good, then, because they reduce the tax debt. Usually, postponement of taxes is also good, and so delaying the "recognition" of gain is usually good, other things being equal. And lowering the tax rate is usually good. This means that if a transaction qualifies for "capital gain" treatment, which is taxed at a lower rate, that's good too.

2. RECOGNITION OF GAIN. The resale of the property, here, occurs in 2015 (January, 2015, but 2015 nevertheless). By shifting the closing into 2015, Edgar Pynes may have shifted the recognition of any gain into 2015, thereby postponing his tax liability.

Whether this shift is desirable depends on other factors. For example, if his income in 2014 was very small and his 2015 income is much bigger, the postponement may not be desirable. But if Pynes puts his money into a new residence promptly, he may be able to avoid current recognition in any event, because the tax laws provide for this.

3. CAPITAL GAIN TREATMENT. Under certain circumstances, gain realized on sale of a capital asset qualifies for more favorable treatment, as capital gain. The requirements include considerations about the length of time the asset has been held. Often real estate deals are structured so that the eventual sale of the property will qualify for capital gain treatment.

4. BUSINESS EXPENSE DEDUCTIONS. If the property were used in a business or held as an investment, the owner would likely be able to deduct additional amounts. For example, depreciation can be figured as an annual amount in accordance with the tax laws and regulations. This amount may be deductible as a business expense. Together with the interest deduction, this depreciation treatment may mean that the property produces paper losses (which are nevertheless real for tax purposes). In this manner, real estate may function as a tax "shelter," providing deductions that can offset income earned from other sources, even as it is actually appreciating on the market—and when it is finally sold, it may qualify for reduced taxation under capital gain principles. (Notice here that Edgar Pynes cannot deduct depreciation, however, because it is not a business expense for him here.)

AN OPTIONAL SHORT FORM ASSIGNMENT FOR THIS BOOK
(TO BE FOLLOWED IF INSTRUCTOR SO DIRECTS)

The following set of page assignments is optional with the instructor. It is designed to reduce the length of required reading in this book, to make it more compatible with courses in which time is at a premium. This version shortens the reading to about **60 pages.**

CHAPTER ONE: Read this chapter in its entirety.

CHAPTER TWO: Omit Sections A (brokerage contract), B (notes and questions on brokerage), and C (negotiations), but do read the Introductory Note preceding Section A, and read the rest of the chapter.

CHAPTER THREE: Read the Introductory Note and the Note on Real Estate Lending Institutions at pp. 17-18. Omit the rest of Section A (loan application). Omit Section C (disclosures). Read the rest of the chapter.

CHAPTER FOUR: Omit Sections I (riders to the mortgage instrument) and J (notes and questions on the riders). Omit the Appendix (covering the FNMA "Limited Payment" Mortgage). Read the rest of the chapter.

CHAPTER FIVE: Read this chapter in its entirety.

CHAPTER SIX: Omit Sections D (undertakings by buyer) and E (disclosures). Omit the Appendix (covering how closing documents are prepared). Read the rest of the chapter.

CHAPTER SEVEN: Omit this chapter.

You should follow the directions given by your instructor. If the instructor indicates that you should use this optional short form, your assignments will not include the matter directed to be omitted. Of course, you are free to read and consider the parts of the book that are designated as omitted, and you may find them interesting, but they are not part of the required reading for the class if the instructor tells you to use this short form.